They Earned Their Stripes

The Detroit Tigers All-Time Team

FROM THE ARCHIVES OF THE DETROIT NEWS

PUBLISHED BY SPORTS PUBLISHING INC.

The Detroit News

Mark Silverman, *Publisher and Editor*
Nolan Finley, *Deputy Managing Editor*

BOOK CREDITS

DETROIT NEWS

Alan Whitt, *Editor*
Richard Epps, *Cover and book design*
Ed Ballotts and Steve Fecht, *Photo Editors*
Chris Farina and Alexander Vida, *Imaging*
Jeff Samoray, *Researcher*

SPORTS PUBLISHING

Tom Bast, *Project Manager*
Vicki Marini, *Project Manager*

Hardcover: ISBN 1-58382-061-2
Library of Congress Number: 00-101661

Published by Sports Publishing Inc.
www.SportsPublishingInc.com

Typefaces: FB Californian, Eldorado, Bureau Grotesque

Printed in the United States

Contents

❖ ❖ ❖

Foreword: *By Alan Trammell*

When I became a professional player, and ultimately a Tiger, all I ever wanted to do was to play for a while. Just give me a few years in the majors, that would have made me happy. I never knew it would be 20 years.

Now to be named to the Tigers' all-time team, I'm extremely honored.

Detroit was a perfect fit for me. Coming from the West Coast as I did, I always viewed the Tigers as one of the traditional teams.

As a kid, I knew all about them and what they had done, like Mickey Lolich coming back on two days' rest in the 1968 World Series against St. Louis and winning Game 7.

I thought of the Tigers as a blue-collar team and that was fine, because I was a blue-collar type of player. I wasn't flamboyant. I just went about my business. I didn't seek attention, I just tried to let my playing do the talking for me.

Sometimes I think it had to be fate. First of all, there was opportunity. How many times are positions open at the same time for a couple of kids as they were for Lou Whitaker and me? We were allowed to learn while playing in the majors. And the fans understood. Somewhere else they might not have.

But that's why Detroit was perfect for me from the start. I wasn't a good player early on, I needed time, but I was young. I'll always be appreciative of how the fans treated me, not just then, but for my entire time in Detroit. It would take forever to say enough thank-you's.

Most of all, I was proud to wear the uniform. Numerous times I'd look down before a game and see that old English D and remind myself of the Tigers' tradition — kind of a timeless style of baseball. I just did

Alan Trammell: "I was proud to wear the uniform."

my job and tried to do it well.

But to be up there with Al Kaline, Charlie Gehringer, Hank Greenberg, that's really something. Great names to be with.

✦ ✦ ✦

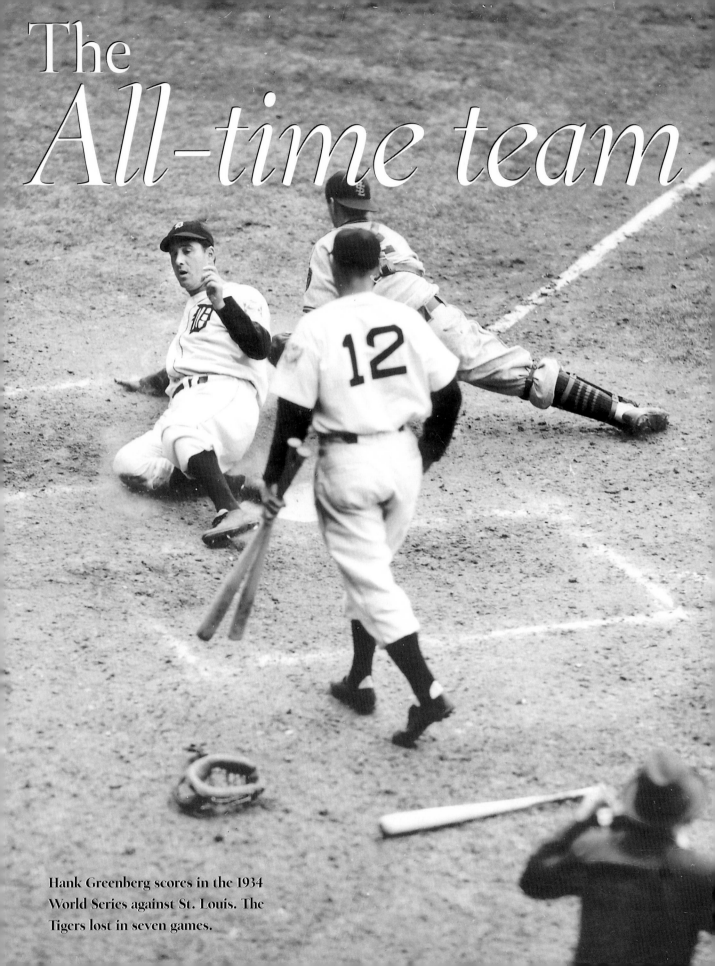

The All-time team

Hank Greenberg scores in the 1934
World Series against St. Louis. The
Tigers lost in seven games.

It began with Cobb, but all-time team took a century to construct

By Jerry Green ✦ *The Detroit News*
FEBRUARY 10, 2000

Tyrus Raymond Cobb arrived in Detroit by train on a steamy August night in 1905. He took a horse-drawn buggy to Ryan's Bed and Board near Bennett Park, which was located on a former haymarket at the junction of Michigan and Trumbull.

Ryan's, it turned out, was the site of a burlesque parlor on the ground floor. The noise kept Cobb awake most of the night. He was drowsy the next day when he reported to Bill Armour, manager of the Tigers.

Armour practiced the same philosophy as Sparky Anderson would three-quarters of a century later. He liked to put a rookie fresh from the minors into the batting order right away. So on August 30, 1905, Ty Cobb, just 18, was listed in the No. 5 spot in the lineup, playing center field. Armour placed Cobb, fresh out of Georgia, in the lineup with Wahoo Sam Crawford, the hitting star of the Detroit club.

The Tigers were playing the New York Highlanders and Cobb had the challenge of facing the best pitcher in the American League in his first game. Jack Chesboro had won 41 games for the Highlanders the previous season.

Between them, Bill Freehan (left) and Al Kaline were named to play in 29 All-Star games.

◆ ◆ ◆

7

In the bottom of the first, Cobb arose from the Tigers' open bench — there were no dugouts at Bennett Park — and with a certain swagger twirled three bats while waiting to bat. Then he stepped in to face Chesboro. The first pitch was a high strike, which Cobb missed. The next was a called strike. Cobb hit the next pitch. He laced it to left center and legged out a double, driving in a run.

A new era had started in Detroit baseball.

All that is baseball in this city — in Bennett Park, then Navin Field/Briggs Stadium/Tiger Stadium and now Comerica Park — is rooted in that day, when Ty Cobb became a major leaguer.

Whatever has happened since, whatever will happen to the Tigers in the 21st Century — it all started on that afternoon, with Ty Cobb.

Baseball is a game of passages, the only sport that can truly be linked from generation to generation. The treasures of the game are passed from grandfather to father to son and then to his son. Or daughter. And granddaughter.

And it is the same for the athletes who comprise the Tigers all-time team — those who have worn the old English D over their hearts. The tradition, the history, have been passed from Cobb to Charlie Gehringer. They were passed onward, from Gehringer to Hank Greenberg to Hal Newhouser to George Kell to Al Kaline to Bill Freehan to Mickey Lolich to John Hiller, and finally, at the end of the linkage, to Jack Morris, Alan Trammell, Kirk Gibson and Sparky Anderson. They represent a century or so of Tigers.

By the time the next all-time Tigers team is announced, who knows what stars will have emerged to replace those great players. Among the current crop of Tigers, none looks ready to join this select group, but who knows?

The current Tigers all-time team — chosen by the popular vote of Detroit's baseball fans in September 1999 — is a collection of superb athletes, including

George Kell, too late on this play, led third basemen in fielding seven times.

four Michigan natives and one adopted son in Kaline. All but one played in at least one World Series in a Tigers uniform. Some possessed overwhelming talent, the "naturals," if you will. Others simply played hard-

time team are:

■ Seven Baseball Hall of Fame members, including Cobb, Gehringer, Greenberg, Kaline, Kell, Newhouser and Anderson.

■ Four batting champions. Cobb won 12 in his 22 years with the Tigers. Gehringer, Kaline and Kell each won one.

■ Two home run champions. Greenberg won it three times, and Cobb once with the magnificent total of nine homers in the dead ball era of 1909.

■ Two league RBI champions. Cobb and Greenberg each won the title four times.

Pitching? Newhouser led the American League in victories in four seasons and was the dominating pitcher of the 1940s. Lolich — a three-game winner in the '68 World Series — and Morris each did it once.

Choosing a Tigers all-time team is a tough task. Through the years there have been many more greats who are worthy, at least, of a spot on the bench of the this all-time team. Sam Crawford, for one, outhit Cobb in 1906. Hughie Jennings, who succeeded Armour in 1907, managed the Tigers to three pennants in his 14 seasons. Much later in the century, all-time team manager Sparky Anderson actually won only one pennant in his 17 seasons in Detroit.

Seventy-five years before Morris arrived, George Mullin was an outstanding right-handed pitcher for the Detroit club from 1902-13.

In the 1920s, as Cobb managed the Tigers and played his final seasons in Detroit, Harry Heilmann became the American League's premier batsman, winning four batting championships.

Any Tigers all-time team begins with Cobb, a mean and nasty person — on the basepaths and on the streets of Detroit. He was detested by opponents. Before every game he would file his spikes to razor sharpness in the clubhouse of Navin Field, the new ballpark that opened in 1912. Then he'd slide into infielders, spikes upraised.

er, or had a mental edge over their peers. Whatever they had, they provided Tigers fans with a museum of memories that is the team's glorious history.

Among the 13 players who make up the Tigers all-

Fowlerville native Charlie Gehringer is one of four all-time team members born in the state of Michigan.

His teammates did not care much for him, either.

Cobb was the player-manager when a quiet, skilled young second baseman from Fowlerville, up near Lansing, joined the Tigers in 1924. His name was Charlie Gehringer. He would play second base for Detroit with simplicity, grace and elegance for 19 seasons.

"He was a tough cookie," Gehringer said a few months before his death in 1993 at age 89, when asked about Cobb. "He taught me a few things that I thought were worthwhile. Then I think I made a wisecrack to him one day, and he didn't talk to me any more, which was a pleasure.

"I didn't dislike him, but he wasn't a nice guy to play for."

That was about as strong a statement as Gehringer

would ever make.

Unlike Cobb, Gehringer was highly respected by the Tigers' opponents. Lefty Gomez, the Yankees' star pitcher, was the one who nicknamed Gehringer "The Mechanical Man."

"That's because the guy is in a rut," Gomez said in a 1930s interview. "You see, he hits .354 on the first day of the season and keeps right on hitting .354 the rest of the season."

Gehringer's highest baseball salary was $30,000. In his days, ballplayers needed to take jobs during the off-season. Gehringer sold baseballs and bats.

"I worked at Hudson's three years during the holidays," he said in a 1992 interview.

Gehringer was the Tigers' bridge between pennant eras. Cobb's Tigers won pennants in 1907, 1908 and 1909, but lost three World Series.

The Tigers would not win another pennant until 1934. By then Greenberg had joined the Tigers, playing alongside Gehringer.

Greenberg, a carefree slugger and a tower of a man, became the Tigers' regular first baseman in 1933.

Catcher Mickey Cochrane, another hall of famer, arrived from the Philadelphia Athletics in 1934 and managed the Tigers to their first pennant since 1909 with a lineup that featured Gehringer, Greenberg, pitcher Tommy Bridges and himself. Still they lost another World Series to the Cardinals.

Then in 1935, the Tigers, at last, won a pennant and a World Series, defeating the Cubs. Goose Goslin drove in the winning run, and he, too, would ultimately qualify for the Hall of Fame. Bridges was the winning pitcher, his second in the Series. And Schoolboy Rowe beat the Cubs in another game.

By the 1935 season, with Babe Ruth departed from the American League and soon from the majors, Greenberg was named MVP, establishing himself as the league's most productive hitter. In 1938, he chal-

Sparky Anderson attempts to stay warm during a mound visit with Jack Morris and Mike Heath.

♦ ♦ ♦

11

Retired John Hiller (right) checks in with two other all-time team members — manager Sparky Anderson and shortstop Alan Trammell — in 1981.

lenged Ruth's single-season home run record of 60 and missed, finishing with 58.

Greenberg liked to spend the mornings before ball-games at Briggs Stadium hitting buckets of baseballs. He'd get high-school kids to shag for him in left field. One of those kids was Mike Ilitch, who later would buy the Tigers.

"I thought he would hit them into the stands," Ilitch said the day he bought the Tigers in 1992. "But he could get them only to shortstop. He soaked them until they were water-logged and so heavy he couldn't get them out of the infield."

Greenberg played for the Tigers until 1946, when they traded him to the Pirates. By time, Detroit native Hal Newhouser had become the best left-hand-

◆ ◆ ◆

ed pitcher in the league. He was a 19-year-old rookie still in high school, when he helped the Tigers to another pennant in 1940. But again, they lost the World Series.

Newhouser, a 29-game winner in his best season, pitched the Tigers to another pennant and their second World Series championship in 1945. Greenberg, released from World War II duty after V-E Day that season, hit a grand slam homer in the final game to clinch the pennant.

With Newhouser in his prime, the lineage of All-time Tigers continued in 1946. The club obtained George Kell to play third base. In 1949, Kell nipped Ted Williams by a fraction of a percentage point to win the batting championship.

In 1953, Al Kaline joined the Tigers, signed for $35,000 off the Baltimore sandlots. Two years later, at age 20, Kaline became the youngest American League batting champion.

It would be another 23 years after the 1945 championship before the Tigers could win another pennant. All-time teamers Kaline, Mickey Lolich, Bill Freehan and John Hiller were part of the 1968 team.

Lolich had been overshadowed by Denny McLain and his 31 victories during the 1968 pennant race. But Lolich, a left-handed pitcher, defeated the St. Louis Cardinals three times in the World Series, outdueling Bob Gibson in Game 7. He remains the last pitcher to win three games in a World Series.

Homegrown catcher Freehan — a tight end at the University of Michigan — used his football abilities to help the Tigers win the series. Freehan's block of the Cardinals' Lou Brock at home plate and tag out on Detroiter Willie Horton's throw in Game 5 turned the Series just when it appeared the Tigers were doomed.

It was the only time in his 22 seasons with the Tigers

Kirk Gibson's attitude and spectacular home runs are the reason Harry Heilmann was eliminated.

that Kaline would play in the World Series. He had refused to attend a World Series game until he played in one.

"It was worth waiting sixteen years," he said sharing a bottle of victory champagne with a Detroit sports writer. "I'd seen other World Series in the country

After hitting two Sunday homers, Charlie Maxwell (center) gets a light from Al Kaline along with pitcher Paul Foytack in 1957.

club, watching on TV. I considered people lucky to be in the Series.

"Our team made a great comeback. We were embarrassed the way we played."

Kaline, before he retired, laced a two-base hit onto the right-field foul line off Baltimore's Dave McNally to become the first American Leaguer to collect 3,000 hits in 49 years. Seven hits later, Kaline retired.

Hiller, in the 1970s, would become the league's premier relief specialist. He saved 38 games, then a record, in

✦ ✦ ✦

1973.

Four other all-time Tigers joined the Detroit ballclub in the late 1970s. Jack Morris came up as a right-handed pitcher in 1977, one year after pitcher Mark "The Bird" Fidrych enchanted America with his antics. With Fidrych injured, Morris became the ace of the staff.

Late in 1977 Alan Trammell was promoted to the Tigers along with Lou Whitaker. They would grace the Tigers' infield for two decades; Trammell, the all-time Detroit shortstop, and Whitaker, a wonderfully talented second baseman.

And then in 1979, Kirk Gibson, the fourth of the Tigers all-timers to be born in Michigan, joined the club, an outfielder-in-training. He had been an All-America football player at Michigan State and played baseball with a football mentality.

Playing with competitive fire and sometimes anger, Gibson was a Tigers' throwback to Cobb.

With Trammell, Morris and Gibson on the club, as young major leaguers, Sparky Anderson was hired as manager in June 1979.

In 1984, Anderson's Tigers led from Opening Day, building a 35-5 start and coasting to the American League pennant. Willie Hernandez, with Sparky campaigning for him, won both the MVP and Cy Young Awards for his supurb relief pitching.

The Tigers trounced the Padres in five games in the World Series, with all-timers Morris, Trammell and Gibson playing key roles. Morris beat the Padres twice with complete-game efforts; Trammell hit two home runs in Game 4 behind Morris' second victory; and Gibson hit two homers the next day to clinch it. Trammell was the World Series

Manager Mayo Smith adds some stripes to Mickey Lolich's jersey in 1969.

MVP with a .450 batting average.

Sparky Anderson sparkled — the first manager to win a World Series in both the American and National Leagues.

So through the years these all-time Tigers have made their mark, winning championships, setting records, making memories and thrilling Tigers fans along the way.

And it all began in 1905, when Ty Cobb touched Jack Chesboro for a double at Bennett Park.

A Century of *Greatness*

Tigers announce their all-time team, Gibson edges Heilmann in outfield

By Tom Gage ✦ *The Detroit News*
ORIGINALLY PRINTED SEPTEMBER 27, 1999

The game has changed since many of them played. George Kell sees his first glove, for instance, every time he goes back to baseball's Hall of Fame. "I don't know how I ever stopped anything with that glove," he said.

But one thing hasn't changed.

"The great players then would still be great players today," Kell said.

And the Tigers' best of yesterday would be stars of today.

Kell would still be hitting doubles into the corner. Hank Greenberg would be hitting upper-deck home runs and Charlie Gehringer would be doing everything right, just as he used to.

Because that's what they did. And that's why their accomplishments always will be remembered.

The Tigers announced their all-time team after more than 25,000 votes were cast by the fans.

As befitting its long history, the players represented all eras of the franchise — from Ty Cobb with no number on his uniform to Alan Trammell, who still looks as if he could play.

Here is the team:

Manager: Sparky Anderson

Native Detroiter Hal Newhouser won back-to-back MVP honors in the mid 1940s.

✦ ✦ ✦

17

Right-handed pitcher: Jack Morris.

Left-handed pitchers: Mickey Lolich and Hal Newhouser (tie).

Relief pitcher: John Hiller.

Catcher: Bill Freehan.

First base: Hank Greenberg.

Second base: Charlie Gehringer.

Shortstop: Alan Trammell.

Third base: George Kell.

Outfield: Ty Cobb, Al Kaline and Kirk Gibson.

The closest voting, other than the tie between Lolich and Newhouser, was at second base and for the third outfield spot. At second base, Gehringer received 51 percent of the votes and Lou Whitaker received 40 percent. For the third outfielder Gibson received 34 percent and Harry Heilmann, a Hall of Fame outfielder who played from 1914-1929, received 23 percent.

But the runner-up team is not too shabby, either.

Manager: Mickey Cochrane.

Right-handed pitcher: Denny McLain.

Left-handed pitcher: None because of the first-place tie.

Relief pitcher: Guillermo Hernandez.

A youthful George Kell checks in at the Tigers clubhouse in 1946.

◆ ◆ ◆

Catcher: Lance Parrish.

First base: Norm Cash.

Second base: Lou Whitaker.

Shortstop: Harvey Kuenn.

Outfield: Heilmann, Mickey Stanley and Willie Horton.

Many of the former players who were on hand for Sunday's tribute to the all-time team also were saying goodbye to Tiger Stadium. For those who grew up as Tigers fans, and always wanted to play in Tiger Stadium — such as Freehan — it was a poignant moment.

"Being from Royal Oak," Freehan said, "I came down here a lot as a kid. And like a lot of kids, I'd go home after the game and pretend to be one of the players I'd just seen."

Freehan went off to the University of Michigan as a two-sport star. As a sophomore, he started in six football games.

"I played both offense and defense," he said. "That's what we did in those days."

But he also batted .585 for the baseball team, a record that still stands.

That was before the baseball amateur draft, so any team that wanted to could knock on Freehan's door after his first season at Michigan. The Kansas City Athletics offered him more money than the Tigers to sign, but there was no doubt where Freehan wanted to play.

"This place had a lot to do with that," he said, looking out from behind the batting cage at Tiger Stadium. "As a kid, I dreamed of playing here. It's bittersweet to see it go. A new ballpark is needed for a lot of reasons, but I loved this ballpark. It's the only one I ever called home."

Tigers manager Ralph Houk presents John Hiller with the Tiger of the Year award Hiller won following the 1973 season.

It was the only one Kaline called home, too, after he signed off the sandlots of Baltimore. But today, he'll see someone wearing his uniform number for the first time since he wore it.

As a tribute to the all-time team members, their numbers will be worn by the Tigers starting at their respective positions — which means that the right fielder will wear No. 6.

"I think it's great they're doing that," Kaline said.

So does Karim Garcia, who will be wearing the number.

"It's an honor," Garcia said. "I'll try to wear it nice."

That's what Kaline did all those years.

✦ ✦ ✦

19

Tiger legends

Hank Greenberg knocked in 183 runs in 1937, one shy of Lou Gehrig's 1931 league record.

Anderson   Greenberg   Morris

Cobb   Gehringer   Newhouser

Kaline   Trammell   Lolich

Gibson   Kell   Hiller

                Freehan

Sparky
Anderson

SPARKY ANDERSON ✦ MANAGER ✦ 1979-1995

Sparky took a young, rudderless team and steered it to greatness

By Lynn Henning ✦ *The Detroit News*
ORIGINALLY PRINTED FEBRUARY 29, 2000

Bedtime is 9 p.m., a couple hours after he has watched ABC World News with Peter Jennings. Wakeup is dawn, or earlier. Then comes a one-hour walk and, later on, a five-minute drive to Sunset Hills Country Club for his daily 10 a.m. tee time and 18 holes of golf with a regular crew of golfing buddies.

His cholesterol level is so crazily low that it sounds as if the numbers must have been transposed: 116. But the good life Sparky Anderson is living these days can hardly be measured by a daily itinerary or by a blood count.

The ex-Tigers manager, who today is expected to be named to baseball's Hall of Fame, has never felt better, or been more at peace. Listen to Anderson crow for a half-hour about the way things are today, compared with the grind that he was enduring a few years ago, and the mystery fades.

He does not miss baseball for the simple reason it was probably killing him.

"My last three years I managed, I was tired all the time," Anderson said, speaking from his home in Thousand Oaks, Calif. "I took a nap every day. On the road, I couldn't miss a day of having that nap.

Sparky Anderson's 2,191 victories is third all-time for managers, with 1,331 coming with the Tigers.

✦ ✦ ✦

Anderson is the only manager to win World Series championships in both leagues.

traveling, eating junk all the time, and not getting the proper sleep," Anderson said. "All those things get those arteries clogged up. You know how that food in the clubhouse is — why, if you ever squeezed the grease out of it, it'd roll into the street."

Five years have passed since Anderson closed the door of his manager's office at Tiger Stadium. Only 61, Anderson had already won more games as a manager than all but Connie Mack and John McGraw, and to this day he remains the lone manager to have won a World Series in both leagues.

Just about everyone in baseball figured Anderson to be back in the game within a year. But after 17 seasons with the Tigers, Anderson was worn out, physically and mentally. The Tigers had been losing regularly since their '80s heyday. And Anderson, now 66, wasn't enjoying the sort of relationship with Mike Ilitch and Co. that he had known under two previous club owners.

So he went home to California, pulled out his golf clubs and the clicker to his TV set, and settled in with his wife, Carol, to the perks of retirement.

The shocker is that he enjoys it. Baseball, he was surprised to learn, was Anderson's passion, but not his life.

"I feel better about myself, because I don't need that (baseball) to get me by," Anderson said. "I find things to do."

Simple things. Amusing things.

Consider the other day's tasks.

Anderson decided after golf had been rained out to not pout and to do something constructive. So he cleaned out his clothes closet. Then he emptied all the drawers in his dresser, got rid of the junk, and

"That's when it started. The way I feel today, I only wish I would have felt this good those years before. I would have stayed managing."

The "it" that started a few years ago, Anderson now knows, was the onset of coronary artery disease. Ashen and becoming more ill by the minute, he hit rock-bottom at Ann Arbor during last July's Millie Schembechler charity golf tournament. A nervous trip to Ford Hospital in Detroit was followed a few days later by heart-bypass surgery.

"They (doctors) think it came from doing all that

Anderson always stood up for his players and he expected a lot in return.

rearranged everything neatly.

Next, he turned to the garage, which in a couple hours was spic-and-span.

Anderson admits there's a satisfaction from these mindless jobs that hadn't been possible during his baseball years.

"It's really changed me," he said. "I'm not lying to you — this is the best I've felt in years. And I have enough sense

now to know that the traveling would still wear me out."

Some trips, anyway. One journey he'll handle is a July 23 visit to Cooperstown, N.Y., where a man who seems as if he was born with white hair will find himself profiled in bronze.

It has been a given for years that Anderson would make the Hall. He took Cincinnati to the World Series four times in the '70s, winning twice as The Big Red

✦ ✦ ✦

Machine came to embody one of the game's great eras.

He picked up with the Tigers, pushing Detroit through a spectacular 1984 season and another world championship. He and the Tigers even squeezed out another playoff appearance in 1987 with a club that looked for most of the season as if it didn't have a chance.

A question has arisen, not that there seems to be any doubt as to its answer: What hat will Anderson choose to wear for his World Series plaque?

There's only one way to go: Cincinnati. The Big Red Machine was a dynasty. It was Anderson's first team. Sparky Anderson became Sparky Anderson as manager of the Cincinnati Reds, a status that persuaded — even required — then general manager Jim Campbell in 1979 to make the temporarily unemployed Anderson an impromptu choice to manage the Tigers.

"It will be the hardest decision I've ever made, because I was treated like a king in both cities," Anderson said. "I had what they'd call a cakewalk — royalty doesn't get the kind of treatment I had with both teams."

But ...

Anderson concedes his Reds teams were a significant slice of baseball history. He also knows that Cincinnati's general manager at the time, Bob Howsam, in 1969 selected a 35-year-old minor-league manager to lead a team on which future Hall of Famers were either then, or soon to be, stacked like bats in a batrack: Pete Rose, Joe Morgan, Johnny Bench, Tony Perez.

Because of his and the Big Red Machine's heritage, Anderson realizes he can wear the Reds hat into Cooperstown and be doing the Tigers no disservice.

"It's a hard thing, but people must understand: It has nothing to do with the hat," Anderson said. "It's a rule of the Hall of Fame that you have to wear it. But you can't go by a hat — you go by what's in your heart."

And Detroit is right there with Cincinnati, Anderson says, persuasively. The town has been in his heart since June, 14, 1979, when he stepped onto the field at Tiger

LYNN HENNING ON SPARKY ANDERSON

He was only 45 years old and already had managed in four World Series, winning two of them. And yet Sparky Anderson was unemployed when Tigers General Manager Jim Campbell approached him in June of 1979.

Nice break for Detroit.

Anderson was hired on June 12, 1979 and managed the Tigers for the next 17 seasons, an astonishing reign of 2,579 games. He won another World Series in 1984, had a 1,331-1,248 record with the Tigers, and retired at the end of the 1995 season having managed more major league games than any other man except Connie Mack and John McGraw.

How Anderson happened to be free when Campbell decided to make a move in June of '79 remains an oddity. Sparky had been baseball's manager of the '70s at Cincinnati, his Big Red Machine winning world championships in 1975 and '76 World Series, after losing the World Series in 1970 to Baltimore and in 1972 to Oakland.

He walked in on a young and rudderless collection of young talent when he arrived at Detroit. But Anderson was a teacher and a psychologist — as shrewd a baseball man as the game has seen. With the Tigers he knew how to meld volatile talents such as Jack Morris and Kirk Gibson with stable, quieter types on the level of Lance Parrish, Lou Whitaker and Alan Trammell.

The 1984 Tigers team was a masterpiece. From a 35-5 start the Tigers were a wire-to-wire sensation, polishing off San Diego in the World Series to make Anderson the first manager in history to have managed a world champion in each league.

He was also friendly, he was a talker, he was a baseball man. There was a decency to Sparky Anderson that was every bit as luminous as his record. It's why he's the Tigers' all-time manager and a certainty for enshrinement in Baseball's Hall of Fame.

Stadium and in his first appearance in a Detroit uniform received a standing ovation that made him shiver.

Part of the reason Anderson feels so torn is that he greeted a core of players in Detroit that would, for all their differences in style and credentials, become part of a relationship Anderson valued as much as anything he had known in Cincinnati.

Alan Trammell, Lou Whitaker, Lance Parrish, Jack Morris, Kirk Gibson. They helped turn Anderson's Tigers into baseball's top team from the '80s, a reign that never overrode the bond that developed between Anderson and his stars.

"He certainly deserves to be (in Cooperstown)," Gibson said last week. "When you put it all together, tell me why he doesn't belong in the Hall of Fame? Can anyone give me a reason?

"Look at what he's accomplished in both leagues, things that put him above all the others who've managed," Gibson continued. "Then, when you see how he loved the game, how he fought for the preservation of the National Pastime. When you look at how good of an interview he was, the way he was an ambassador to the game, what he did for his players. ...

"I can truly say he could have sent me down the road, he could have given up on me, but he cared for me, also."

Anyone who thinks for a moment baseball has separated itself completely from Anderson's life, or that it has been tucked like a golf sweater into one of those closets Anderson cleaned out the other day, is missing the gist of how Anderson's days have changed.

Baseball is there, all right, like a kind of boarder in the Anderson household. He talks frequently with his neighbor, Mike Scioscia, the Anaheim Angels manager.

He watches games, selectively, but religiously — as a manager would watch.

"Last year I really loved watching Cincinnat-uh," he said, giving that Mason-Dixon twist to the final syllable. "Cincinnat-uh, to me, they were

"You know how I feel about Sparky. It's been an honor to play for him. Those who didn't want to play for Sparky had a different agenda. They weren't team-oriented."

KIRK GIBSON
on playing for Anderson

Manager: Sparky Anderson 1979–1995

He gave the Tigers 17 years of effective managing, winning two division titles and a World Series. He was one of the game's most colorful characters.

He was a sidewalk philosopher:

"I can't believe they pay us to play baseball — something we did for free as kids."

"I don't know why the players make such a fuss about sitting in the first-class section of the plane. Does that mean they'll get there faster?"

"Don't call us heroes. Firemen are heroes."

Anderson is the only manager to win a World Series in each league.

Sparky profile

Anderson spent 17 seasons in Detroit to become the team's career leader in victories. ... Won World Series championships with both the Tigers and Cincinnati Reds. ... Also is only person to be the winningest manager for two teams (Tigers and Reds). ... Third on all-time managers list in career victories (2,194), behind Hall of Famers Connie Mack and John McGraw.

refreshing, the way they went about it. Jack (McKeon, Reds manager) did a tremendous job with that club.

"The Yankees, I always enjoy watching them, too, because I think (manager) Joe Torre — whether people know it or not — he got that club to play very professionally. New York is probably the most professional club in the major leagues and, let me tell you, when he first went there, those guys were outlaws.

"But you know who's a really good manager? Bobby Cox," Anderson went on, talking about the man who annually takes the Atlanta Braves to a division title and who, too often, misses out on a grand prize. "Don't ever be fooled by those World Series or playoff games.

✦ ✦ ✦

Ah, the art of managing

According to the world of George Anderson, there are several components to managing:

1. "I never wanted to be a manager, but I always studied the game, even as a kid. I just wanted to be a better player, not a manager. I used to steal signs for Charlie Dressen when I played for him in Toronto in the 1960s. He called me aside in Syracuse one day and said, 'You're going to be a manager.'

"He said if I wanted to know anything about managing to come to him, but not until the next day. I didn't know what he meant but then I realized he wanted to figure out things for himself before I asked him any questions."

2. "I managed Toronto in 1964 but I thought that was it. I was selling cars that winter — not many of them, you understand — when I got a call and was told to report to Rock Hill in the Western Carolina League in 1965. That's where it really started. My first day in camp, they had all the managers together in a meeting and asked them how they planned to do things that season. They all had something different to say. When they got to me, I told them I couldn't tolerate what they were saying. I was saying we should all do things together and do them the right way. I guess they liked that and they put me in charge of all the other managers. So how did I start with my team? We won five and lost 25."

3. "I did OK as time went on. That's because I had props. It's the only way to manage. You've got to have props. One night we were getting beaten in Savannah. I kept slipping balls into my pockets. I had three of them tucked away. I called a

Sparky's managerial record

In the World Series

Year	Team	Opponent	W–L
1970	Cincinnati	Baltimore	1-4
1972	Cincinnati	Oakland	3-4
1975	Cincinnati	Boston	4-3
1976	Cincinnati	New York	4-0
1984	Detroit	San Diego	4-1

The all-time greats

Manager	Wins	Losses	Pct.
Connie Mack	3776	4025	.484
John McGraw	2840	1984	.589
Sparky Anderson	2194	1834	.545
Bucky Harris	2159	2219	.493
Joe McCarthy	2126	1335	.614

Tops with the Tigers

Manager (years)	Wins	Losses	Pct.
Sparky Anderson (1979-95)	1331	1248	.507
Hughie Jennings (1907-20)	1131	972	.538
Bucky Harris (1929-33, 55-56)	516	557	.481
Steve O'Neill (1943-48)	509	414	.551
Ty Cobb (1921-26)	479	444	.519

meeting the moment the game was over and I threw one ball at a swinging door in the clubhouse, just missing a pitcher's head.

"I told them, 'Boys, I have two more to throw. Does anyone in this room want to die?' I got their attention and told them I'd kill them if they didn't come to the park to win."

4. "My philosophy? The first rule, and thank God I learned it in my very first year, is you have to have the players to win. The most important thing is to be honest with them. If you do that, they'll be yours. But if a player finds you've lied to him, you'll not only lose him but 10 others in the clubhouse. I also believe calling players by their names. It's so important to them, and it's easy to do.

> *"I never wanted to be a manager, but I always studied the game, even as a kid. I just wanted to be a better player, not a manager."*
>
> SPARKY ANDERSON

◆ ◆ ◆

Anderson was big with the fans, especially after the Tigers won the World Series in 1984.

The 1984 season

"I know this will sound crazy because we won everything, but 1984 was my hardest year in baseball. When we got off to that 35-5 start, I began to worry. What if we lost it? What if we blew that lead?

"Trying to stay in front became an obsession with me, and I didn't enjoy things the way I should have.

"I knew what was driving me but I didn't talk about it. I wanted to show Cincinnati it was wrong to fire me. I was consumed by this thought. I wanted it more than anything else. I wanted 1984 for myself.

"I was literally shot by the end of the season. I almost quit, figuring I'd won in each league and what else was there to do. You'll never know the relief I felt when Gibson hit that big home run in the final game against San Diego."

◆ ◆ ◆

Farewell Sparky

ORIGINALLY PRINTED OCTOBER 3, 1995

Detroit Tigers Manager Sparky Anderson has resigned after 17 seasons. While he was in the dugout, Detroiters witnessed some special moments.

It is easy to talk about Sparky's accomplishments, especially since he is the third winningest manager in Major League Baseball history. He won two World Series with the Cincinnati Reds before landing here in 1979.

Back then he nurtured a youth movement that eventually led to a Tigers championship in 1984. It was a storybook season in which the Tigers led the division from start to finish and manhandled its opponents in the playoffs.

As good as that season was, Sparky rightly considers 1987 his best moment. A team he figured no better than a fifth-place finisher made the playoffs. The team, helped by the pivotal late-season acquisition of pitcher Doyle Alexander, took the Blue Jays to the final day of the regular season and won the division.

But what made Sparky stand out is his character. He always seemed forthright with the fans and the press. That quality came through during his resignation speech on Monday, when he publicly upbraided himself for being "obnoxious" to a member of the media following his last game on Sunday.

Sparky usually showed his better side.

He genuinely seemed to care about others and gave generously of his time with the press and fans. And his charitable efforts were further testimony to that spirit. Sparky also worked well with players. He showed patience. He didn't rely much on gimmicky clubhouse meetings. He just insisted that certain standards be maintained, and they included players working together.

Anderson considered 1987 his best moment with the Tigers, not the championship year of '84.

He gave his players the credit when the team won and shouldered the blame when it lost.

Unfortunately, the Tigers have done a little too much losing during the past four seasons. The team is now dedicated to rebuilding itself with younger players who will take time to develop.

◆ ◆ ◆

Sixto Lezcano (16) gets into it with Anderson in 1980, who denied having his pitcher throw at Lezcano.

At age 61, Sparky says it is time for a change. So he is bowing out to give the team and himself a chance to pursue their own best interests. He may manage another team. Call the resignation a gesture that may eventually allow both the team and Sparky to flourish again.

Sparky Anderson has left an indelible mark on Tiger baseball. He is popular not only because of his overall winning record, but more importantly because of how he conducted himself on the job. Change is difficult, but sometimes it is for the best.

We hope that this farewell turns out to be a bright new beginning for both the Tigers and Sparky.

◆ ◆ ◆

Ty
Cobb

Ty Cobb ✦ Outfield ✦ 1905-1926

Cobb dominated baseball with his keen mind and a will to succeed

By H.G. Salsinger ✦ *The Detroit News*
Originally printed November 2, 1924

I n any all-time rating of players, Tyrus Raymond Cobb stands alone. He was the greatest of the greats, a fiery genius and the game's outstanding individualist. Brilliant and unorthodox, he made baseball history for more than two decades. He dominated the game.

He gained his pre-eminence not because he was the fastest base runner, nor the best base stealer, nor the fleetest fielder or the leading hitter but, because he had the nimblest brain that baseball had known. He had the ability to perceive a situation and take full advantage of it before his opponents became aware of it. He was a keener student of the game than his contemporaries and understood the game better than they did. What is more, he understood them better than they understood themselves. He knew their playing faults and weaknesses and he also knew their strengths.

His wide edge over the field was mental. He thought more quickly than any rival, and he put his mechanical skill to more uses than they did. Many of his hits were attributed to superior speed, but the explanation does not hold since several others were as fast but they did

Ty Cobb sits in the stands of Briggs Stadium with Walter Briggs on June 29, 1941.

not cause fielders to hurry their throws the way Cobb did. They did not cause infielders to fumble and make wild throws the way Cobb did. They did not upset infields the way Cobb did.

✦ ✦ ✦

33

Cobb saw the game unlike any of his contemporaries. He always seemed to be two plays ahead of the game.

His is the story of a mighty brain and the driving force of genius that made him great when other men, superior in physical strength and natural ability and speed, remained mediocre.

He was the greatest player because he thought ahead of them at all times. The play directly in front of him was not his aim, but the play that was to come after. The play of the moment, until he scored, was merely the foundation for the play that was to come.

He was not the greatest fielder, for a dozen men in baseball towered over him as outfielders. He was not the greatest place hitter, for "Wee Willie" Keeler was a bit better in placing hits. He was not the greatest slugger, for a few dozen men have been able to hit a ball harder than Cobb ever could. He was not the fastest man in the game, for several others were fast, a few even faster.

In baseball, having speed and knowing how to apply it are different things. Cobb knew better how to apply it than other men just as fast. Cobb could have been trained to run straight-away and would have made a remarkable sprinter. But his biggest asset as a

♦ ♦ ♦

sprinter was his break from the jump.

In base running, his brain work was as conspicuous as his speed. He started before they expected him to start. He went when they did not expect him to go and he made no attempt to advance when he was expected to. He always crossed them up.

Nearing a bag, Cobb's next move was always figured out. He knew exactly what he wanted to do. More than that, he was certain of what the other fellow would do. That made it easy for him to act. He knew how to escape the fielder.

Cobb was not the hitter that the sluggers of the old school were, not in the strict sense of the word. And he was never a natural hitter. But Cobb made more hits than the men naturally fitted for hitting, again because of his brain. He thought faster than the pitcher. As he knew the workings of an infielder, of an outfielder, so did Cobb know the system of the pitcher he was opposing. He batted accordingly.

He did not use mystic powers. He had no occult gifts. He simply reduced baseball to a scientific basis and figured it out accordingly. Cobb's plays may appear mystifying, but they only resembled a conjurer's tricks. The feats of a magician are astounding and beyond comprehension until they are explained.

Then they become extremely simple. Cobb's play was always just as simple.

Once explained by him, once he gave the reason for making the play the way he did, it became clear and simple. Analyzed, most great achievements become reduced to the same simple, comprehensive level.

He thought faster than any man who ever wore spiked shoes. And he thought more thoroughly. He saw the little things that the others missed and he took advantage of them. Nothing escaped his observation. The mechanical performances of a fielder, the minute physical characteristics of a pitcher, were studied by Cobb, analyzed by him and then used as

George Cantor on Ty Cobb

The plaque on the outside wall of old Tiger Stadium said it well: "A genius in spikes."

Tyrus Raymond Cobb was all of that. Although time has changed the game he played and erased several of his records, his accomplishments still place him among the greatest hitters and the most talented of all Tigers.

He studied the mental dynamics of the game as thoroughly as any man who ever played. He understood the uses of intimidation and fear. He sat in the dugout sharpening his spikes to sow the seeds of doubt and seemed to insinuate himself into the minds of his opponents.

Although not the fastest runner, Cobb could take over a game on the bases by unnerving the other side. Although not the most natural hitter, he always found the gaps in the defense, the weakness in the opposing pitcher's makeup.

His only speed was hyper-aggressive. He fought everyone with an equal degree of antagonism — teammates, fans, opponents. Tigers catcher Charlie Schmidt became a team hero because he beat him up in a clubhouse fight. But when Cobb was suspended for going into the stands and attacking a fan, the entire team went on strike in support.

He was an avowed racist and probably the most hated ballplayer of his era. He never won a championship, which gives his critics room to disparage his achievements.

But in the first two decades of the 20th Century, he stood alone at the pinnacle of the game — a genius in spikes and a tiger in spirit as well as uniform.

the basis of his attack. He built his offense against the weak points of their defense.

There has been but one Cobb. There is likely never to be another. In him were strangely combined all those qualities that were needed to make the perfect competitor, a man with playing faults but with the most highly developed competitive spirit and the finest developed brain that the national pastime has produced.

❖ ❖ ❖

Ty Cobb's secret: A hope he cherished

By H.G. Salsinger ✦ *The Detroit News*
ORIGINALLY PRINTED NOVEMBER 2, 1924

Ty Cobb is recognized as one of the greatest hitters of all time. But his secret ambition was to become a pitcher.

As a boy he played on the infield, at short. But the ambition of every boy who likes base ball is to be a great pitcher. That was the secret ambition of Cobb.

Never during his years in baseball had Cobb become fully convinced that, had he concentrated upon pitching, he could not have become one of the greats of the game.

He brought his ambition with him to the majors and he nursed it through all these years. Whenever he could enlist the services of a catcher Cobb practiced pitching.

He would work with the catcher for half an hour or more, generally more. And while he worked, Cobb pitched twice as many balls as any regular pitcher would in the same length of time, for Cobb pitched as he played, with a nervous speed.

He managed to develop what players describe as a "dinky hook," meaning an amateurish curve ball delivery. He never was able to pitch a real fast ball and what he called his slow ball was ineffective because of faulty delivery.

Players who looked over Cobb's pitching were never impressed by it, and this hurt Cobb's pride. The result was that he tried all the harder. One brilliant spring day in 1909 in San Antonio, Tex., where the Tigers trained, Cobb had recruited a catcher and was having his morning workout pitching.

The late Herman Schaefer, then a veteran and wise in the ways of baseball, walked over to Cobb and said to him:

"Listen! Take a piece of advice from me and cut out this monkey business. Forget that you are a pitcher.

Outfielder: Ty Cobb 1905-26

Cobb had two great beliefs as a player: 1. The bat is a wondrous weapon. 2. The base line belongs to me.

He was the game's greatest hitter and maybe its greatest competitor. He fought everyone, the opposition, his teammates, on and off the field. He was an imposing guy who asked no favors and gave none.

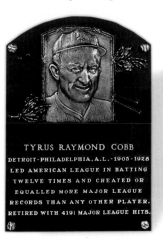

He looked for every edge. For instance, he did not eat after the games. He was too wound up. He would go back to his hotel room and try to unwind, even take a little nap. Only then would he go to dinner. No meat, either. And he wouldn't eat lunch because he felt he could play better on an empty stomach.

Cobb was the first player to swing more than one bat as he waited to hit. He was hard to handle, and as a youngster he would stand in center field and munch on popcorn. He would often steal second, third and home in the same inning — doing it once on three straight pitches.

Cobb highlights

Inducted into the Hall of Fame in 1936. ... Nicknamed "Genius in Spikes" because of his competitive nature. ... Owns highest career batting average in baseball history at .367. ... Second on baseball's career hits list (behind Pete Rose) with 4,191 hits. ... No. 1 in career runs with 2,246. ... Also ranks second in triples (295), fourth in doubles (724) and fourth in stolen bases (892). ... Batted better than .400 three times, including a .420 average in 1911 when he won the Chalmers Award as the American League MVP. ... Won A.L. batting title 12 times in 13 seasons between 1907 and 1920. ... Won triple crown in 1909 with a .377 average, nine home runs and 107 RBI. ... Led Tigers to World Series

You ain't. You can never be one.

"You've been pitching for four years that I know of an' you ain't got no more stuff than a high school boy. There's a lot of good pitchers and there's a couple of thousand that's

Cobb's career .367 batting average is tops in baseball and his 4,191 hits is second only to Pete Rose.

Ty Cobb's statistical career

Year	AB	R	H	HR	RBI	Avg.
1905	150	19	36	1	15	.240
1906	358	45	113	1	34	.316
1907	605	97	212	5	119	.350
1908	581	88	188	4	108	.324
1909	573	116	216	9	107	.377
1910	506	106	194	8	91	.383
1911	591	147	248	8	127	.420
1912	553	119	227	7	83	.410
1913	428	70	167	4	67	.390
1914	345	69	127	2	57	.368
1915	563	144	208	3	99	.369
1916	542	113	201	5	68	.371
1917	588	107	225	6	102	.383
1918	421	83	161	3	64	.382
1919	497	92	191	1	70	.384
1920	428	86	143	2	63	.334
1921	507	124	197	12	101	.389
1922	526	99	211	4	99	.401
1923	556	103	189	6	88	.340
1924	625	115	211	4	78	.338
1925	415	97	157	12	102	.378
1926	233	48	79	4	62	.339

better than you'll ever be but there ain't a lot of outfielders with good throwin' arms and my advice to you is: quit the tryin' to be a pitcher an' save your arm for the outfield."

Cobb did not take the advice. Instead he tried harder to prove that Schaefer and the others were wrong. He never proved them otherwise than right, but while he continued pitching, Cobb wore out his arm. It gradually weakened, and baserunners, quick to observe the weakness, took advantage of it.

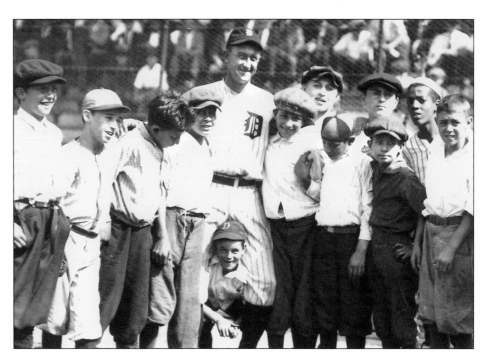

Cobb wasn't always surly, here posing with members of a boys baseball team.

❖ ❖ ❖

Cobb raised a ruckus away from field

By Doc Greene ✦ *The Detroit News*
ORIGINALLY PRINTED JULY 18, 1961

Ty Cobb has been called variously a "fiery genius of the diamond," the greatest ball player who ever lived, the "immortal of baseball" and many other justifiable things, none of which can be contested in any great degree.

He had another side, and in all honesty I have never heard any of his intimates say wholeheartedly and without reservation, "I liked him."

His career, especially in the early days, was spotted with trouble on and off the field — much of it of his own making.

The "fiery genius" hit an elderly Negro asphalt worker on Woodward Avenue when the laborer asked him not to walk on his freshly poured cement.

A warrant was issued but later quashed. The first man admitted into the Baseball Hall of Fame got into a fight with a night watchman in the Euclid Hotel in Cleveland and used a knife on him.

The case went to a grand jury. The Detroit Baseball Co. spent more than $1,000 to extricate the "greatest ballplayer who ever lived" from this one.

The Georgia Peach entered a meat market at 1526 Hamilton, operated then (1914) by one William Carpenter, waved a loaded .32 revolver and declared someone "has insulted my wife." The hassle turned out to be over a purchase of 20 cents worth of perch.

A boy named Howard Harding, Carpenter's wife's brother, tried to protect the proprietor and finally the pair went outside. Cobb handed the revolver to one bystander, his hat to another and proceeded to beat up the youngster.

He dislocated his thumb in the process and was removed to Bethune Station in a patrol wagon. Tyrus eventually pleaded guilty to a charge of disturbing the peace and was fined $50 by Justice Stein after Carpenter preferred charges.

His attorney, James O. Murfin, in entering the guilty plea, said, "Cobb regrets this incident to the bottom of his being. He regrets it exceedingly on account of the management of the Detroit team and his teammates. He feels that as they are struggling along he should be in the game and giving them his assistance, particularly as they have been loyal to him in the past.

"Cobb believes he made a mistake and has promised that he will control his temper in the future. He has learned his lesson."

At one time he caused the entire Detroit ball club to be turned out of the Copley Square Hotel in Boston over alleged improper conduct.

On another occasion he was ejected from the Chicago Beach Hotel for using improper language to a clerk in the presence of women guests. He became infuriated when manager Hughie Jennings would not move the entire club, quit the team and returned to Detroit.

He attacked a newsboy named "Scabby" Barnes over a crap game in the Detroit clubhouse. Soon after that he was accosted by two men on the way to the depot one evening and stabbed in the back.

He never offered any explanation. In 1925 he was arrested for disorderly conduct after an argument with a waitress in Augusta, Ga., over the size of a luncheon check.

He told the intervening policeman to "run along and peddle your papers." The patrolman didn't comply and Cobb wound up at headquarters. He subsequently was fined.

✦ ✦ ✦

Cobb owned the baselines, and catchers paid the price if they stood their ground.

President of the American League Ban Johnson once demanded Ty's resignation as a manager because of the way he treated his players, remarking, "He ought to be training Marines at Parris Island, the way he handles players."

And there is neither time for nor point in recalling the numerous altercations in which Cobb found himself aggrieved by umpires, fans and what all during the actual pursuit of baseball.

◆ ◆ ◆

39

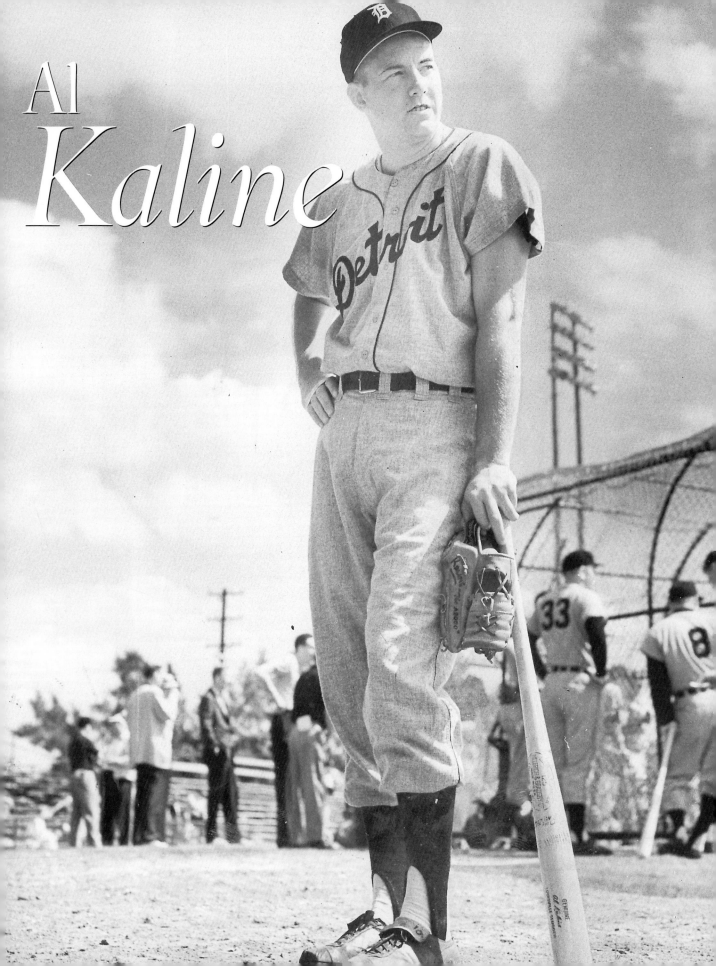

Al *Kaline*

Al Kaline ✦ Outfield ✦ 1953-1974

The 'can't-miss' kid became a man, earned respect right before our eyes

By Joe Falls ✦ *The Detroit News*
Originally printed January 13, 1980

Nothing was happening. It was one of those hum-drum days in Lakeland that seemed to last forever. Yet, it was only 11 o'clock in the morning.

Jack Tighe, who was the new manager of the Tigers, was sitting on one of the benches at Tigertown, where the rookies and minor leaguers and a few of the regulars off the Tigers were going through one more endless day of throwing the ball, hitting it and picking it up.

"You know something," said Tighe, "he can't miss."

"Who can't miss?"

"Kaline," he said. "By the time he is done, they'll have him in the Hall of Fame in Cooperstown."

"Sure. He can't miss." The reply was tinged with more than a touch of sarcasm.

How could anyone say any ballplayer would achieve the game's highest honor after only 3 ½ seasons in the business. Preposterous. Tighe, the old bald-headed codger, was playing his games again. It was his first year on the job, and if he got No. 6 on his side — and that was always tough to do — it would make it a lot easier for him. It could give him a little job security.

Al Kaline waited 16 seasons to finally collect a World Series ring with the Tigers.

✦ ✦ ✦

Kaline never spent a day in the minors, going straight from high school to the majors in 1953.

It could even make him a good manager. When No. 6 was on his game, he was something special.

But No. 6 wasn't always on his game. Sometimes he sulked. Sometimes he loafed. Sometimes he wouldn't talk to you at all.

It was the spring of 1957, and Kaline was still growing up — still trying to find his place in the world.

Strange as it is to say in the glow of all his glory, but there was a time when Al Kaline was not a very pleasant person to be around.

He threw helmets. He threw bats. He threw tantrums. It wasn't easy moving into such a fast-paced world when you grew up in the Westport section of Baltimore, where the fields were made of dirt and only

♦ ♦ ♦

dirt and the whole world was nothing more than row houses upon row houses upon row houses...

By the time he was 18, he was in the major leagues.

By the time he was 20, he was the American League batting champion — the youngest in history. Younger, even than Ty Cobb.

What did he know? What could he know? All he had ever done was go to school and play baseball. There was no time for anything else. No time for girls.

No time for growing up.

So he was a simple man with simple tastes. He didn't drink, he didn't smoke, he didn't even chew. Fancy foods didn't interest him. Nor did fancy clothes.

He never spent so much as a minute in the minor leagues. So he never learned how to pack a suitcase, send out his laundry...or even how to order dinner.

They rushed him right to the big leagues because his raw talent excited them.

They wanted to refine it themselves. They wouldn't trust anyone else. His first days in Detroit were the most difficult of his life.

"I lived in the Wolverine hotel," Kaline recalled, "and it really scared me. It was the first time I had ever lived alone and I didn't know what to do with my time.

"We didn't play many night games — 14 or so — and so I was off almost every night. I'd go to the movies a lot or just walk around the streets looking in the store windows.

"It seemed like it was always 10 o'clock at night and I had nothing to do. I didn't even know who to talk to."

He couldn't wait until the mornings. He was up early, for a quick breakfast, and on his way to the ball park before they even opened the dressing room door.

The ball park was his sanctuary. He could feel comfortable there. He could sit around in his underwear and hone his bats or beat on his glove. It felt good to be in the dressing room even if nobody else was around.

"I used to wear the same clothes every day when I

George Cantor on Al Kaline

There are so many plays over Al Kaline's long career, but the one that remains in my mind was just a simple fly ball to shallow rightfield.

After a long and exhausting battle with Boston, the Tigers were just one out from clinching the American League East pennant of 1972. Kaline had come back from an injury late in the year and the team was riding his bat down the stretch.

Now on an early autumn evening in a packed Tiger Stadium, the ball was lifted to right and Kaline came loping in, waving his arms. It was a signal that it was finally going to be all right, that the old master had it all under control.

That was what Kaline meant to this team and this city for more than 20 years. A standard of excellence that we eventually took for granted until it was gone.

He played the outfield's most demanding position impeccably, with the sort of grace that makes sportswriters sound like balletophiles. He was the last man an opposing pitcher wanted to see at bat with the game on the line.

If he had hit one more home run in his career, he would have been the first player with 3,000 hits and 400 homers. But the stats don't begin to tell the truth. This was one player you truly had to watch day after day to understand how gifted he was.

He came here as a skinny kid from Baltimore and remained to become one of the best loved symbols of Detroit. To those of us who grew up in the 50s, he was the Detroit Tigers, and he remains a token of that lost time and place; forever young and running gracefully free.

lived at home," he said.

"I'd wear a pair of jeans three or four days in a row, and the same shirt and the same shoes. Who knew the difference?

"Now I could see how the other players were dressing — different suits every day. A different shirt. A different tie. Here I am with only one suit and I'm wearing it day after day."

Kaline demonstrates one of his many all-around skills with a theft of home in September 1957.

The embarrassment became so heavy that at night, he began staying in his hotel room and listening to the radio.

There were no TV sets in those days so he would just sit there and "sort of think about things."

He finally went out and bought himself a couple of sports coats.

The toughest part was dealing with the sports writers. At breakfast in the coffee shop, he didn't have to talk to anyone. He could bury his head in the newspaper. On the way to the ballpark, he could walk briskly and keep his eyes straight ahead.

But after the games, the writers would come around with their questions and he didn't know how to handle them.

In fact, they didn't know how to handle them. This was the major leagues, so he had to be a major leaguer.

Al Kaline's statistical career

Year	AB	R	H	HR	RBI	Avg.
1953	28	9	7	1	2	.250
1954	504	42	139	4	43	.276
1955	588	121	200	27	102	.340
1956	617	96	194	27	128	.314
1957	577	83	170	23	90	.295
1958	543	84	170	16	85	.313
1959	511	86	167	27	94	.327
1960	551	77	153	15	68	.278
1961	586	116	190	19	82	.324
1962	398	78	121	29	94	.304
1963	551	89	172	27	101	.312
1964	525	77	154	17	68	.293
1965	399	72	112	18	72	.281
1966	479	85	138	29	88	.288
1967	458	94	141	25	78	.308
1968	327	49	94	10	53	.287
1969	456	74	124	21	69	.272
1970	467	64	130	16	71	.278
1971	405	69	119	15	54	.294
1972	278	46	87	10	32	.313
1973	310	40	79	10	45	.255
1974	558	71	146	13	64	.262

◆ ◆ ◆

44

Wrong.

"They really scared me," said Kaline. "I didn't even know why they wanted to talk to me. I was no hotshot or anything. I'd had a few articles written about me in the Baltimore papers, but nobody ever came around to interview me. Now the writers were coming around all the time and they were asking me all kinds of things and I didn't know what to do about it."

So he ran. He ran to the shower, to the trainer's room and sometimes right out of the ballpark.

This didn't sit well with the writers, who were only thinking of themselves and their stories. They began painting the new kid as being hard to handle, rude, discourteous and even stuck on himself.

So this was the public portrait of young Al Kaline: A talented kid who didn't know how to handle his success.

It never was an easy game for him — not when he won the batting championship in 1955 and not when he became an accomplished veteran in later years.

It was always a struggle. He had to fight for his hits and he had to extend himself to make all of those marvelous catches and all of those cannon-like throws.

He asked more of himself than anybody, and on the days when he didn't meet his own standards, he became angry.

He became angry with himself and angry with anyone who approached him.

He slammed his bat to the ground in digust. He threw his helmet into the dugout in fury. Sometimes his frustration got so intense that he forgot where he was or what he was supposed to do and he wouldn't run out a ball or he'd pull up short of the bag.

This was the cardinal sin. Loafing. It was really kid's stuff, but nobody knew it, not even Kaline himself, and so the writers came down on him harder than ever.

"I just never thought I should make an out," he said. "I thought I should get a hit every time up. I didn't know how to handle it."

Outfielder: Al Kaline 1953-74

He didn't think he would ever be a hitter, so as youngster in Baltimore — the son of a broom maker — he worked on his fielding and became one of the greatest right fielders in history, ranking with Roberto Clemente.

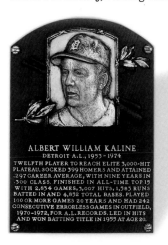

And yet, in his second season with the Tigers, he won the American League batting title with a .340 average. He got a $15,000 bonus for signing, not the $35,000 which appeared in the newspapers.

Kaline suffered many injuries in his career but was still one of the most consistent players in the game. Much was made of the time he turned down a $100,000 contract, giving back $8,000 because he felt he hadn't earned it. Little known was the fact that when he got his 3,000th hit, owner John Fetzer gave him 3,000 silver dollars.

Kaline profile

Inducted into the Hall of Fame in 1980, Kaline batted .297 with 3,007 hits and 399 home runs in his career with the Tigers. ... Won the American League batting title in 1955 with a .340 average at age 20, the youngest in league history. ... MVP runner-up in 1955 and 1963. ... Batted .379 against he Cardinals in 1968, with two homers among his 11 hits. ... Played in 18 All-Star games. ... Hit .300 or better eight times and hit 20-plus homers nine times. ... An outstanding defensive player, he won 16 Gold Gloves and had a streak of 242 consecutive errorless games. ... First Tiger to have number (6) retired.

He broke into a grin.

"That's what happens when you are young," he said.

The maturing process was slow. His lofty standards held him back more than anything else. It took him a long time — almost 10 years — before he began to realize that every man has his limitations, even himself.

Even when he played in his 2,000th game, his manners left something to be desired. When the reporters

Kaline was often misunderstood during his quest for perfection ...

came around to his locker to get his sentiments about reaching this milestone, he was abrupt with them.

He didn't think anything of his accomplishment. All it meant to him is that he had put on his uniform 2,000 times.

The difference is that later he realized his mistake in being so rude. He sat there and said, "Damn, damn, damn...I did it again. Why did I act that way?

"I should have understood what they wanted.

✦ ✦ ✦

Would you please apologize to them for me?"

As a kid, nobody asked him questions about anything. He had simply been able to do almost anything on a ball field. In four years in high school he batted .333, .418, .469 and .488.

All he wanted — summer and winter — was to play baseball. His parents saw his love of the game and encouraged him at every turn.

"They didn't even want me to work," said Kaline. "I had a job in a drugstore, but they wanted me to quit it so I could play baseball. I remember them telling me one day, 'You will be old for a long time and you'll have to work for a long time, so enjoy your games now.'"

As he spoke now, Kaline was sitting on the sofa of his den in his home in Bloomfield Hills. He was looking out the window.

"Looking back now, I can see how much my parents meant to me," he said. "My dad worked in a broom factory and he walked to work. He'd come home for lunch and go back again. At the time I was in elementary school, my mom was also working. She worked in a whisky distillery rolling barrels up into freight cars.

"I was aware of all this because my dad and I used to pick her up after work.

"She would be wearing overalls and we'd pick her up at 5 o'clock. My mom was very strong. She never complained about anything. She was the strongest one in our family. Even though she was a little woman, she was stronger than my dad.

"Actually, she had two jobs. She would come home and cook dinner for us and then she'd go downtown with some other women to scrub floors in bank buildings. We would pick her up again at 11 o'clock and she was always so happy to see us."

Young Al Kaline never had any money, but he never needed any. He never even thought about money. He'd go to the movies once in a while, but most of the time he was playing ball.

... punishing himself more than anyone if he didn't meet his own standards.

When the Tigers signed him in June of 1953, they gave him $15,000 in salary to be spread over 2 ½ seasons (or about $1,000 a month) and a $15,000 bonus, which he turned over to his parents so they could pay off their home.

Near the end of his playing days, the ritual was always the same whenever the Tigers were riding the bus in from Friendship Airport in Baltimore.

Al always sat on the right side of the bus. That's so he could see the three smoke stacks just behind Cedley Street in Westport.

He said the same thing all the time: "There it is, guys...my old home town! We lived right over there, behind the powder factory. A great place to grow up."

In private moments, when he was driving into town with his wife and two sons, he would always go past the smoke stacks. He wanted his boys to see where he lived, where he grew up as a boy. "I wanted them to know that life was never always easy," said Al Kaline. "I want them to know you had to work hard to get ahead."

◆ ◆ ◆

Kirk
Gibson

KIRK GIBSON ✦ OUTFIELD ✦ 1979-1987, 1993-1995

Gibson's numbers not spectacular, but his pure willpower thrilled us

By Joe Falls ✦ *The Detroit News*
ORIGINALLY PRINTED NOVEMBER 16, 1988

You always knew he was around. He might be screaming at someone in the clubhouse — he did that a lot. Or he might be grousing around the batting cage.

He did that a lot, too. Or he might be cussing out traveling secretary Bill Brown on the team bus. He did that a whole lot.

You could not ignore Kirk Gibson. You were always aware of his presence.

It was that way on the field. He might be doing nothing more than leaning over on his knees and waiting for the next pitch. Or he might be playing catch with the center fielder, making those long, lazy throws from his position. You always found yourself watching him.

I think all the players felt the same way about this man. It didn't matter if he was on your side or if he played against you. You knew where he was and what he was doing. He commanded this kind of attention because you never knew what he was going to do.

The anticipation was always very sweet with Kirk Gibson.

Gibson was a man who reached everyone around him because if he did anything at all, you knew it would be special.

You knew it would be big. It might be a strikeout followed by a raging fit of anger. Or it might be a towering drive off the third deck in right followed by a wild tour around the bases.

You watched him all the way because you didn't want to miss anything.

The temptation of his detractors is to measure him by numbers.

"Yeah, but he hit only .290."

"Yeah, but he hit only 25 homers."

"Yeah, but he batted in only 76 runs."

How can a guy with figures like that win the MVP award?

These comments come from those who know this man only from a distance. You have to get close to him

✦ ✦ ✦

49

to understand him. You have to see him, touch him and smell him. You have to look into his eyes and see the rage. You have to hear it in his voice. It can be very frightening, especially when he is out of control.

Kirk Gibson is a bully, and there are no redeeming qualities to a bully. When he was with us, he pushed people around all the time. He would tell you in his quieter moments that he considered himself a good man. On many occasions, he was. But too many times he mistreated others, usually those who were defenseless.

But again, you could not ignore him.

He forced you to become a part of his world and it could be a very irrational world. It could get violent at times. He always gave off this heat, this searing emotion that was always welling up inside of him, and you could feel it in every part of the ballpark.

The reason Kirk Gibson is more than another ballplayer is that when he reaches inside of himself for extra strength, he forces others to reach inside themselves.

He makes everyone react to him. He is an exceptional athlete because he brings out things in others that normally would remain dormant.

We know of Gibson's stirring homer in Game 1 of the 1988 World Series. That one will live forever. It was one of the great moments in the history of baseball.

But even more revealing were the two home runs he hit against the Mets in New York during the playoffs.

Those two reached everyone on his team in a way that was truly inspiring.

Everyone in Dodger Stadium went wild over his World Series homer. That was easy to do. It was a clean and clear moment.

But in New York, where his teammates were struggling for survival, this man gave them a life when they didn't think they had one. He showed them there was

LYNN HENNING ON KIRK GIBSON

Kirk Gibson was a ninth-inning pitcher's nightmare. To see Gibson approaching the plate with a game on the line in Detroit's final at-bat was to feel as if a movie director had taken control.

Something dramatic was about to happen.

He hit so many theatric home runs during his baseball career, 12 of his 17 seasons having been spent in Detroit, that heroic at-bats became an expectation. His defining moment as a Tiger came during the fifth game of the 1984 World Series, when he homered twice as Detroit mopped up San Diego to win the world championship.

Gibson's second homer that day came against an old villain, Goose Gossage, in Detroit's final at-bat. It was a perfect climax to an extraordinary year of baseball in Detroit, and it helped lend a certain permanency to Gibson and to his legacy as a Tigers star of enormous color and excitement.

He was an outfielder who had staggering size and speed, a perpetually scruffy three-day beard, and a snarl about him that telegraphed to all the world that he meant business.

And when he departed Detroit for the Los Angeles Dodgers in 1988, no one in these parts was surprised that Gibson would take his heroics with him, homering in the 1988 World Series to give the Dodgers a first-game victory in what has been called the most dramatic World Series home run of all time.

a way when none seemed to exist. He showed them what pure willpower could do.

Kirk Gibson is now the most valuable player in the National League. The verdict is correct, but it will not sit well with some people around here.

Go back to Feb. 1. That's when he walked out of Detroit. When he left, only a few complained. Only a few were upset. It was mostly a case of good riddance.

He was never my favorite person, but like everyone else, I could never take my eyes off him.

◆ ◆ ◆

Rejuvenated Gibson revved up Tigers

By Jerry Green ◆ *The Detroit News*
Originally printed May 9, 1993

Kirk Gibson's statistical career

Year	AB	R	H	HR	RBI	Avg.
1979	38	3	36	1	4	.237
1980	175	23	113	9	16	.263
1981	290	41	212	9	40	.328
1982	266	34	188	8	35	.278
1983	401	60	216	15	51	.227
1984	531	92	194	27	91	.282
1985	581	96	248	29	97	.287
1986	441	84	227	28	86	.268
1987	487	95	167	24	79	.277
1993	403	62	105	13	62	.261
1994	330	71	91	23	72	.276
1995	227	37	59	9	35	.260

Imagine this make-believe scene as Sparky Anderson meets the media in his little office in the Tigers' clubhouse.

Reporter: "How about the new guy?"

Sparky: "He's gonna be great, he runs fast as anybody I ever seen, he can hit for distance and let me tell you what a great attitude he brings into this clubhouse."

Reporter: "Who's he remind you of?"

Sparky: "To me, he's gonna be another Kirk Gibson, indeed.

"He's different, but he isn't," Anderson said. This statement was delivered in a genuine scene in the office, not make-believe. "He's every bit as intense, but he's more controlled intense."

A few days earlier, Anderson had opened his regular pregame radio show on WJR by saying: "I always felt Gibson belonged in Detroit. Like some players belong in L.A., Cincinnati, New York, Gibson was Detroit."

It was an admission of a mistake, not Sparky's, that contributed to the ruination of the Detroit baseball franchise. Sparky did not complain then.

But now, in his clubhouse, he told a reporter: "Certain people should never leave certain places. In my opinion, Lance Parrish, Kirk Gibson and Jack Morris never should have left Detroit. It's like Willie Mays never should have left the Giants or if Ted Williams played for Detroit."

Gibson is back from his trip around major-league baseball. He's rejuvenated, older, leaner, his face cleanly shaved, his attitudes and work-ethic infectious, his batting average soaring above .380.

And unexpectedly, the Tigers — a team doomed to oblivion in preseason estimates — have spent much of early 1993 in first place. They have been winning, they have been fun, they have been, at times, electrifying.

"I don't think it's fair to say I'm the guy who created that," Gibson said about the changed attitude of the Tigers. "That has to come from my teammates."

But Gibson's impact has meant a spot in the pennant race. His teammates confirm that.

"I think I have a positive impact, yes," said Gibson, seated in the old clubhouse, "But so do a lot of other guys. But I fit in well. There's a mesh.

"I'm here to be a world champion. I said that when I signed. Everybody looked at me like I'm nuts. Nobody thought we'd be where we are now. But I talked as if we would be here."

The stereo fired away with hot stuff and strange lyrics in the raucous clubhouse. The shouts and curses of Gibson could be heard above it, punctuating the bedlam in the room. The Tigers had won that night. Gibson had been a factor in two rallies with two sweet singles. One of them was hit sharply to left field.

Gibson had come home again, the same, yet different. It seemed a bit like 1984.

Once upon a time, Gibson was Anderson's vision of

◆ ◆ ◆

the next Mickey Mantle. It was another of Sparky's raves and it damaged the prospect. But eventually the prospect became a player, and if he never matched the heroics of Mantle, he was uniquely Gibson.

He swore an angry streak, played with a face full of three-day bristles, and developed a love-hate relationship with the fans in his hometown. He played with the mighty knack of hitting home runs when they were vital to his ballclub. And the Tigers won the World Series in 1984 with him a feature player.

Then he went away in a contract dispute with management. The owner of the ballclub, Tom Monaghan, said good riddance and that he was a disgrace to the Tigers uniform. A lot of people said the same thing.

It was a horrific mistake — for the ballclub.

Gibson, who believes it is unwise to say what is better left unsaid, declined to fire back. Instead, he proved the folly of his owner by leading the Dodgers, his new team, to another pennant and then hit another historic home run to turn a World Series.

Now after five years of exile and temporary retirement, Gibson is home, in the clubhouse, in the dugout, helping restore pride in the old English D the Tigers wear on their home uniforms.

Across the room, the newcomer, Gibson, was playing cards with his Detroit teammates. He would shriek at times, in words that cannot be printed; he always did. He would get up and stomp around. He always did.

On the field, in batting practice, he would swing mightily, miss and emit a mouthful of terrible words audible throughout the ballpark. He always did that, too.

"I think he makes people realize they are better than they really are," Sparky said.

He always did that, too.

But he is different. With the thinner body and the whiskers off his face, he is, maybe, a tad mellow at age 36, pushing toward 37.

And believe it or not, the batting stroke is different.

Outfielder: Kirk Gibson 1979-87, 1993-95

He did not have big numbers. He had a big heart. Sparky Anderson, who managed for 26 years in the majors, said he never had a player who delivered more clutch home runs than this man.

His home run and war dance around the bases in the 1984 World Series might have been the most dynamic moment in the history of the Tigers. And he hit a winner for the Los Angeles Dodgers in the '88 World Series that was even bigger.

He was not a good fielder and had trouble throwing the ball. But it didn't matter because he played all-out every moment on the field. He set a standard for his teammates that made them better players. He gave off the sparks and they caught fire.

Gibson profile

The former Michigan State football star's dramatic home run in the clinching game of the 1984 World Series cemented his reputation as a clutch performer. ... He was the first Tiger with 20 home runs and 20 stolen bases in the same season. ... Was the American League championship series MVP in 1984. ... Is sixth in club history in stolen bases and 10th in home runs. ... After stints with Los Angeles, Kansas City and Pittsburgh, Gibson returned to the Tigers in 1993 and retired in 1995.

Only two other players from the '84 champions remain in this clubhouse in '93 — Lou Whitaker and Alan Trammell, two Tigers for life.

And it was Trammell who first pointed out the difference in Gibson's batting approach.

Trammell was always a student of the game, of its moods and nuances. The day Gibson left the Tigers, forced out by the former regime, to sign with the Dodgers, Trammell summed up the serious loss for his ballclub. He said the Tigers would be losing their fire, the influence Gibson had in the clubhouse, creating a football-style atmosphere.

Now Trammell observed Gibson and said:

"He's had a great impact on our club in the middle of the lineup," Trammell said. "He's brought back a different dimension. He's not striking out as much as he did. He's a better hitter. He's going the other way."

◆ ◆ ◆

Kirk Gibson will always be remembered for this Game 5 home run against San Diego's Goose Gossage, clinching the 1984 World Series for the Tigers.

◆ ◆ ◆

PLAYERS ONLY

nk
reenberg

Hank Greenberg ✦ First Base ✦ 1930, 1933-1941, 1945-1946

Greenberg's grace under pressure made this Tiger baseball royalty

By Joe Falls ✦ *The Detroit News*
Originally printed September 5, 1986

Hankus, Pankus. He was large. He was lumbering. He was a laborer. He was ours. Detroit's. Nobody had one like him and nobody ever will. You get only one Hank Greenberg in your lifetime. They taunted him in those early years. This was in the Depression when Detroit was on its knees.

He came to us as a gawky, gangling youngster out of The Bronx in New York. The other teams saw his potential and power and called "Jew Boy" from the corners of the dugouts.

The Yankees were the worst. He would not sign with them and now, fearful of his awesome ability and what he could do to them with his bat, they tried to shake his confidence with their slander.

We didn't have blacks in baseball in those days, so they picked on the ethnics — the Italians, the Poles, the Irish and the Germans. It was the way it was in the Depression.

"They reserved a little extra for me because I was Jewish," Greenberg said. "They got pretty vicious. One time the Yankees even brought up a player from the minors just to get on me. He sat next to the manager for protection. I heard it all from them — every slur

Tigers home-run hitters Rudy York and Hank Greenberg provided a one-two punch in 1938.

✦ ✦ ✦

55

Hank Greenberg watches his 30th home run sail out of the park against Cleveland on August 3, 1935.

you could think of."

Hankus Pankus had the perfect answer for them — another liner into Section 14, lower deck, left field. That was his place in the 1930s and later, after the war, for a short time in the 1940s.

It was the only way he could silence his attackers, but it wasn't easy for him.

It wasn't easy because baseball was never easy for this man, even though he became the greatest slugger in the history of baseball in Detroit — a Hall of Famer who towered over his peers for nearly a decade.

He had to work for what he got, but that's the way it was in Detroit in those days. Everyone had to hack out a living, even the cleanup hitter for the Tigers.

He would come out early, before the ballpark was open, and collect the kids in the streets. They knew where to be, and when, and what big No. 5 needed from them.

◆ ◆ ◆

He brought them into the big ballpark and they spread out through the outfield and he would hit baseballs at them until the blood ran off the end of his bat.

Hank Greenberg was an honest worker in a time of trial in Detroit and his perseverance inspired our city in ways that raised the spirits of those who saw him perform.

The city had Joe Louis and Jack Adams and Dutch Clark and Hank Greenberg and it was important — because the city didn't have much else. These men gave Detroit a reason to feel proud.

From his earliest days, Greenberg was special. He had style, as well as desire and determination. He dressed well and spoke well and commanded attention wherever he went. You could tell it was No. 5, in or out of uniform. They knew him along Michigan and Trumbull — and this was in the era before television. They played during the day in the 1930s, which meant the evenings were free for the players. Greenberg would always try to have a fine meal for himself, even if it meant he had to come up with 50 cents or more to pay for it. "I remember the Statler Hotel used to have a full-course meal for $1.25, and every night you'd wrestle it over in your mind whether you should pay that much for dinner," he recalled. "I went there one night and they had the prettiest waitress I ever saw, so I went back there for a week straight — at $1.25 a night — before I had the courage to ask her for a date." If this man is to be remembered for anything besides those majestic shots into Section 14, it was his royal and regal manner. Whether he was jogging around the bases with those bulky pants billowing in the afternoon air or ordering a filet for his guests at the Beverly Hills Tennis Club, he did it with a flourish.

When they retired his number, along with Charlie Gehringer's No. 2, we went to see him in Beverly Hills to do a piece for our paper. This was three or four years ago. Doc Holcomb was along to take the pictures and

JERRY GREEN ON HANK GREENBERG

The baseball season of 1935 was the start of the proudest, most diverse sports championship reign of any city in America. Led by Hank Greenberg, A.L. MVP, home run and RBI champion, the Tigers won the World Series for the first time.

In quick succession, the Lions won their first NFL championship and the Red Wings won their first Stanley Cup championship. Two years later, Joe Louis won the heavyweight championship. Detroit was renowned across the nation as The City of Champions.

Greenberg became the most productive hitter in the American League in the wake of Babe Ruth's departure. He hit 39 homers and drove in 170 runs in championship '35. In 1937, he had 183 RBI, one off the record of Lou Gehrig in 1931. In 1938, Greenberg made a captivating bid to match or break Ruth's historic record of 60 home runs in a season, set 11 years earlier. He finished with 58.

In 1940, he led the Tigers to another pennant with 41 homers, 150 RBI and .340 batting average.

Then he was one of the first major leaguers go off to the Army and ultimately into World War II.

Captain Hank Greenberg was released from the military near the end of the war. It was just in time for him to help the Tigers to another pennant. On the final day of the season, he hit a grand slam homer. The Tigers continued on to beat the Cubs in the World Series.

He was elected to the Hall of Fame in 1956.

we showed up in the middle of his tennis match. Right away, you could see he was involved in the game. He waved to us to sit down and went on playing. He excused himself from the court and came over and shook hands and led us to an umbrella-shaded table. He motioned to the waiter and said, "Give these men whatever they want," and hustled back on the court.

He must have been 70 or 72 at the time, and his age was showing. He was slightly stooped over and the flabby skin on his legs had fallen over the top of his

❖ ❖ ❖

Greenberg receives the Most Valuable Player plaque from judge Kennesaw Mountain Landis on July 24, 1936.

knees; the flesh bounced as he ran around the court.

He wore a blue L.A. Dodgers cap, and even though it shaded his face, you could see the fire in those eyes as he went after each ball. He kept up a running conversation with himself:

"Dammit!" "Hell!" "Bleep!" "Bleep!" The profanity

Hank Greenberg's statistical career

Year	AB	R	H	HR	RBI	Avg.
1930	1	0	9	0	0	.000
1933	449	59	135	12	87	.301
1934	593	118	210	26	139	.339
1935	619	121	203	36	170	.328
1936	46	10	18	1	16	.348
1937	594	137	200	40	183	.337
1938	556	144	175	58	146	.315
1939	500	112	158	33	112	.312
1940	573	129	195	41	150	.340
1941	67	12	18	2	12	.269
1945	270	47	84	12	60	.311
1946	523	91	145	44	127	.277
1947	402	71	100	26	74	.249

never stopped, and you knew in that instant why he was such a great ballplayer. He could not allow himself to be second best.

As a kid growing up in New York, he wanted to be a ballplayer, while his dad wanted him to be a lawyer or a doctor — or something of true merit. But the game of baseball pulled in the young Henry and he thought of little else in those early years in The Bronx.

He could hit the ball a great distance but catching it was another matter. Running the bases with the gangling frame was difficult. But he never stopped trying to learn.

He'd go to the butcher shop after school and con the owner out of a pail of sawdust. He would spread it over the front yard of his house and practice sliding all afternoon.

The real problem would come later on. That's when his dad got home from work. Young Hank couldn't clean up all the sawdust, and his father would look at the mess and chastise his son.

This became almost a nightly ritual, but in time the elder Greenberg understood his son's needs and desires — and soon he was batting a few balls to him in front of the house.

Greenberg will be remembered for many things. His

Greenberg played in four World Series with the Tigers, winning in 1935 and '45.

58 homers. That rainy day in St. Louis when, just out of the Army, he hit that home run into the left field seats in the ninth to wrap up the pennant for the Tigers. He'll even be remembered for taking the money and running — $125,000 (a staggering figure in those days) for one final season with the Pittsburgh Pirates.

But this sports writer, who grew to love this man in his later years, will remember him for that day in the press room in Comiskey Park in Chicago. It was a Sunday morning in 1956, the writer's first year on the beat with the Tigers and his first trip to Chicago.

Greenberg was the general manager of the Sox. When he came into the room, the young reporter slid down in his seat at the mere sight of this great man.

He seemed so tall, so tanned, so terribly important.

First base: Hank Greenberg 1930, 1933-41, 1945-46

A demon worker, he would take batting practice until his hands bled from holding the bat. He loved batting in runs more than anything else. He would tell Charlie Gehringer, who batted ahead of him, "Charlie, just get 'em around to third. Just third. I'll drive them in."

After a night game in Briggs Stadium, Greenberg was so unhappy with himself he had them turn the lights back on and took batting practice until 1 a.m.

As a kid learning the game, he did not know how to slide and spread sawdust all over his father's lawn and practiced day after day. He hoped his father was too tired from work to notice the mess his son made.

His greatest disappointment was when he hit 58 home runs in 1938 and missed tying Babe Ruth's record of 60. With five games to go, the St. Louis Browns walked him four times in one afternoon.

Greenberg profile

Inducted into the Hall of Fame in 1956. ... Drove in more than 100 runs seven times and hit better than .300 eight times. ... Played in four World Series with the Tigers, winning championships in 1935 and 1945. ... Was American League MVP in 1935 and 1940. ... Had 183 RBI in 1937, one short of Lou Gehrig's A.L. record. ... Hit 58 home runs in 1938, tied for fourth-best in A.L. history. ... Has a career .605 slugging percentage, fifth-best in baseball history. ... Tigers retired number (5) in 1983.

As the young writer looked down at the table, he heard a soft voice: "Hi, aren't you Joe Falls of the *Detroit Times*? I'm Hank Greenberg of the White Sox. It's a pleasure to meet you." Greenberg offered his hand to the young writer. It was the first time on the beat anyone had called the young writer by his name.

One of a kind.

Charlie *Gehringer*

CHARLIE GEHRINGER ✦ SECOND BASE ✦ 1924-1942

Gehringer was a Rembrandt who made game look easier than it was

By Jerry Green ✦ *The Detroit News*
ORIGINALLY PRINTED JANUARY 22, 1993

Detroit Tigers Hall of Famer Charlie Gehringer, considered by some to have been the greatest second baseman of all time, played the game with simplicity, grace and elegance.

At the time of his death at a Bloomfield Hills nursing home in January 1993, Gehringer was the oldest living member of the Baseball Hall of Fame, and a Tiger for 19 years. He lived to be 89 years old.

Born in Fowlerville, Mich., he was baseball's prototype second baseman for the Tigers from 1924 until 1942, when he left for naval service during World War II.

He was a teammate of Ty Cobb's in Detroit and a longtime opponent of Babe Ruth and Lou Gehrig. He bridged baseball generations — playing with Hank Greenberg after Cobb left Detroit, and against Ted Williams, Joe DiMaggio, Lefty Grove, Bob Feller and Lefty Gomez.

After baseball, Gehringer served as general manager of the Tigers for several seasons in the 1950s. He had several times rejected the opportunity to manage the Detroit ballclub.

Gehringer was a young ballplayer off the farm when he joined the Tigers late in the career of the immortal Cobb, the club's player-manager. Cobb was a man who never endeared himself to opponents and teammates alike.

"He was a tough cookie," Gehringer reminisced last July in an interview with the *Detroit News* at the home he shared with his wife, Jo in suburban Beverly Hills.

"He taught me a few things that were worthwhile. Then I think I made a wisecrack to him one day, and he didn't talk to me anymore which was a pleasure...

"I didn't dislike him, but he wasn't a nice guy to play for."

The statement was about as strong as Gehringer would ever make. He was known throughout his career and after it as a man who preferred silence to talking. He was always neat, well-groomed in public, properly attired on the golf course, where he played regularly this past summer as he approached 90.

✦ ✦ ✦

LYNN HENNING ON
CHARLIE GEHRINGER

Ty Cobb, who had an opinion or two about major-leaguers of his time, once said that, along with Eddie Collins, Charlie Gehringer was "the greatest second baseman I ever saw."

Not many would have argued with Cobb on that one. Gehringer was magic. Great bat, graceful fielder, consummate team man.

He was a small-town Michigan boy from Fowlerville who had such a long and lustrous career that in 1949 he was voted into the Hall of Fame. Gehringer's statistics are stunning. A left-hand batter, he hit .300 or better in 13 of his 16 seasons. He had 200 or more hits in seven of those seasons and ended his career with a .320 lifetime batting average.

He also had good power for his day, especially for a man who was only 5-foot-11 and 180 pounds. Gehringer six times hit 15 or more home runs and in seven seasons had 100 or more runs batted in. In 1936, he had an astonishing 60 doubles.

He was also at the heart of Detroit's 1935 world championship and its World Series berths in 1934 and 1940. He was the American League's Most Valuable Player in 1937 and was runner-up to his teammate Mickey Cochrane in 1934.

"The Mechanical Man," they called Gehringer, a player of such efficiency and skill that he remains to this day one of not only Detroit's, but the game's all-time greats.

Charlie Gehringer had a quiet grace, never wasting words off the field or swings of the bat on it.

Baseball was a different game in Gehringer's era. He was a left-handed batter with a sweet, smooth swing. He batted .320 over his career, winning the American League batting championship with a .371 average and winning the league's Most Valuable Player Award in 1937.

He was the pillar of three pennant winners in Detroit, in 1934, 1935 and 1940. When the Tigers won Detroit's first world championship in 1935, Gehringer batted .375 in the six-game World Series with the Chicago Cubs.

"We won one out of three," Gehringer said of his World Series years during the July interview. "In 1934, we got beat by the Cardinals. The Dean boys (Dizzy

♦ ♦ ♦

Thrilling threesome: Lou Gehrig, Gehringer and Joe DiMaggio were three of the big bats of the 1930s.

and Paul) hammered us."

But in that tumultuous seven-game World Series with St. Louis, Gehringer batted .371.

The sports writer who knew Gehringer best was the late H.G. Salsinger, longtime *Detroit News* sports editor.

In 1937, the year Gehringer won his batting championship, Salsinger wrote in his *News* column:

"Naming Charlie Gehringer the most valuable player in the American League is conferring a belated honor upon one of the immortals of baseball, but honors have always been late in reaching Gehringer. He has had 12 complete seasons in the major leagues and as early as 1930, he was acknowledged, by his own professional brethren, to be the best infielder in the game, but not until two or three years ago did the public begin to appreciate him...

"Vernon (Lefty) Gomez nicknamed Gehringer 'The Mechanical Man.'...He rarely ever spoke on the field,

Second base: Charlie Gehringer 1924–42

The Quiet Man. He never liked a fuss. He signed his name "Chas." Gehringer because, "Why use seven letters when four will do?"

An exceptional hitter, he also was a graceful fielder in his 19 years with the Tigers from 1924 through 1942.

They said he never spoke a word. "Not true," Chas said. "If somebody asked me a question, I would answer them. If they said, 'Pass the salt,' I would pass the salt."

When the city held a civic banquet for him, he got up and said: "I'm known around baseball as saying very little, and I'm not going to spoil my reputation." He sat down and the party was over.

Gehringer profile

Inducted into the Hall of Fame in 1949. ... American League MVP and batting champion in 1937, and finished runner-up to teammate Mickey Cochrane for MVP in 1934. ... Played in a club-record 511 consecutive games between (1927-31). ... Batted at least .300 13 times, with more than 200 hits seven times. Compiled a career .320 batting average. ... Played in World Series in 1934, 1935 and 1940, winning Tigers first championship in 1935. ... served as Tigers general manager (1951-53). ... Tigers retired number (2) in 1983.

on the bench or in the clubhouse.

"One time Pat Malone was having an argument with Gomez when Malone insisted that Bill Herman, then with the Cubs, was the best second baseman in the game but Gomez insisted that Gehringer was top man.

" 'But he's such a colorless guy. He's just a mechanical player,' said Malone."

" 'Yeah, I guess you're right,' admitted Gomez, 'but that's because the guy is in a rut. You see, he hits .354 on the first day of the season and keeps right on hitting

Ty Cobb shakes hands with Gehringer in 1939.

Charlie Gehringer's statistical career

Year	AB	R	H	HR	RBI	Avg.
1924	13	2	6	0	1	.462
1925	18	3	3	0	0	.167
1926	459	62	127	1	48	.277
1927	508	110	161	4	61	.317
1928	603	108	193	6	74	.320
1929	634	131	215	13	106	.339
1930	610	144	201	16	98	.330
1931	383	67	119	4	53	.311
1932	618	112	184	19	107	.298
1933	628	103	204	12	105	.325
1934	601	134	214	11	127	.356
1935	610	123	201	19	108	.330
1936	641	144	207	15	102	.354
1937	564	133	209	14	116	.371
1938	568	133	174	20	96	.306
1939	406	86	132	16	107	.325
1940	515	108	161	10	86	.313
1941	436	65	96	3	46	.220
1942	45	6	12	1	7	.267

Call to the Hall was a well-earned honor

ORIGINALLY PTINTED MAY 7, 1949

Those of us who have been present on the many afternoons when Charley Gehringer was as much magician as ball player are gratified but not at all surprised that he has been voted into Baseball's Hall of Fame in a landslide.

Charley was the Rembrandt of the second sack, with an art so polished as to conceal its art.

Nature endowed him with superb equipment for the game and a set of reflexes so instant that the right play ceased to be a conscious process.

Very early he had so mastered the mechanics of infield play that he could go from there and and give it style, the extra something that marks the great from the merely competent, the Heifetz from the fiddler in a tavern.

It was the same with hitting. Here and there in the league are still batters, and very good ones, whose style is so patently Gehringer's as to leave no doubt of its inspiration.

As with many an artist, his genius registered first on the knowing ones, his colleagues. It was only after the word sifted out from fellow players and discerning scribes that the public assayed Charley at his true worth.

Gradually it dawned that no one else was doing or could do what Charley did routinely.

The game's great include many second basemen; but none was a greater joy to watch than our Charley, or more rewarding to those required to report on the pastime — the writers who were in no doubt that he belonged among the immortals. After all, perfection is about as good as you can get.

♦ ♦ ♦

Gehringer's offensive production helped lead the Tigers to three World Series appearances.

Player's favorite, too

By Schoolboy Rowe

Originally Printed September 6, 1954

I suppose people will think I'm prejudiced in picking Charlie Gehringer as my all-time favorite. Prejudiced or not, I have to go for the old Mechanical Man. I used to get a kick out of just watching him in batting practice.

Charlie was the most graceful player I ever saw. He was a great team man. On the hit and run, he was tops. I never saw his equal as a second baseman, and I've been kicking around the big leagues for 20 years.

One day in '35, I was pitching against the White Sox. Going into the eighth inning, we had a one-run lead. They filled the bases with one out. Next up was Al Simmons, one of the toughest hitters I ever faced.

Simmons smashed one back through the box that almost tore my leg off. It looked like curtains but Gehringer saved us with the greatest play I've seen. He came out of nowhere and, half-falling, made a backhand save. With his gloved hand, he tossed to Bill Rogell to start a double play that got us out of the inning.

◆ ◆ ◆

Alan *Trammell*

ALAN TRAMMELL ✦ SHORTSTOP ✦ 1977-1996

Trammell's consistency moved him ahead of Rogell at shortstop

By Jerry Green ✦ *The Detroit News*
ORIGINALLY PRINTED JULY 3, 1988

The dream was first. The urchin scrabbles through the hole in the fence to sneak into the big-league ballpark. The lad fields on the rock-strewn pitches of the sandlots, then the lumpy high school diamonds and at last the dry-grass fields of the bus-trip minors.

"I get joy from this game, I do, I really do," Alan Trammell says. "This is my life. Baseball is my life. I don't know what I'd be doing if I didn't play baseball. I graduated from high school. I signed and three days later I was in Bristol, Va. Playing minor-league baseball.

"My dream was to make the major leagues."

He has played for the Tigers 11 seasons. He has been the most valuable performer in a World Series. And he has been to the brink of breakdown, denigrated by his own manager, stuffed into deep despair.

Some maintain he is the best pure ballplayer in the game today. His manager, Sparky Anderson, was the first to say that: "The best player in baseball right now."

The music rocks from the stereo in the Tigers' clubhouse. It is before the ballgame. Alan Trammell's left elbow is strapped top and bottom. He cannot play this day, the result of a pitch that hit him point blank on the elbow. But he has been on the field, working at his position. He has tried to swing in batting practice. It hurts. Pain does hurt him. But he keeps doing his work.

He sits at his locker. The face is somewhat older now, at age 30. It carries the look of the veteran. For the first time, you notice there is a slight receding at the hairline. But the joyous look, really, it is unchanged from the first time you saw him, when he was 19, the kid from San Diego. A rook fresh from the minors.

The word is ego. Reggie Jackson had it in barrels full. Peter Rose had it by the ton. Sparky has it. Boggs, Brett, Mattingly, Winfield. You can see their egos on their uniforms. Some swagger with it. They glow.

"I don't consider myself that type of player," says Alan Trammell. "I think Alan Trammell being consid-

✦ ✦ ✦

67

Trammell won four gold gloves at shortstop.

Alan Trammell's statistical career

Year	AB	R	H	HR	RBI	Avg.
1977	43	3	8	0	0	.186
1978	448	49	120	2	34	.268
1979	460	68	127	6	50	.276
1980	560	107	168	9	65	.300
1981	392	52	101	2	31	.258
1982	489	66	126	9	57	.258
1983	505	83	161	14	66	.319
1984	555	85	174	14	69	.314
1985	605	79	156	13	57	.258
1986	574	107	159	21	75	.277
1987	597	109	205	28	105	.343
1988	466	73	145	15	69	.311
1989	449	54	109	5	43	.243
1990	559	71	170	14	89	.304
1991	375	57	93	9	55	.248
1992	102	11	28	1	11	.275
1993	401	72	132	12	60	.329
1994	292	38	78	8	28	.267
1995	223	28	60	2	23	.269
1996	193	16	45	1	16	.233

"I'd rather talk about the ballclub. I've always tried to be a team player. I never thought about or dreamed of being a clean-up hitter regardless of where I played. I never batted clean-up, even when I was a kid. I always thought of myself as a table setter."

Alan Trammell did not bat clean-up until last season. Lance Parrish had left. Sparky was groping for run production. He had one of his hot flashes at spring training.

"I don't know what he saw in me," Trammell says now. "At first I thought it was one of those things. Like the Chris Pittaro thing."

Sparky says things in the spring. In the spring of '85, Sparky tinkered with a championship ballclub. He tried to move Lou Whitaker, Trammell's second-baseman partner since the minor-league days, to third base. Pittaro was the best young infielder he'd ever seen, Sparky declared. Etched in cement. The experiment cracked up all over Sparky.

ered one of the better players is enough. Sparky put me in the clean-up spot and I did some things. Most people look at offensive statistics and that's why I'm getting some recognition.

"I don't want to change my make up. That's not me. I'd be a phony. I don't want to change.

"I heard Sparky, *Sports Illustrated*, say I'm the best. I want my playing to do the talking. I'm not going to go me...me...me...I...I...I.

◆ ◆ ◆

The spring training of '86 was the one at which Sparky uttered his immortal line: "Pain don't hurt you."

Alan Trammell was the object of Sparky's scorn. He had damaged his shoulder. In the spring the shoulder hurt when he threw to first base. His mind flooded with self-doubt.

Sparky nagged him. Then one day, on the bench of the spring park in Fort Myers, Fla., Sparky delivered his comment. It translated into something about playing with pain. The words hurt Trammell, too. He complained that mind-games were being played with him.

"All during '86 spring training my shoulder was killing me," Trammell now says. "I was very discouraged going into the season.

"I didn't know how I was going to make it. Thoughts went through my mind that I wouldn't play shortstop again.

"I worried so, I didn't want them to hit the ball into the hole because I didn't have it. I couldn't throw them out.

"I was thinking about this each day. Constantly. Baseball is my life. I went from being on the top — a World Series hero — to a time when my belief that I was a bona fide major-league shortstop was dwindling.

"I didn't know how to handle it."

He played the first half of the '86 season with this mental agony. His shoulder ached. He was never certain he could make the throw across the infield. His statistics dwindled with his belief.

One day Sparky talked to him. Sparky told him there'd be no more criticism, told Trammell just to play the game whichever way he wanted.

"Halfway through the season, everything was OK," Trammell says now in the clubhouse of a his first-place ballclub.

"And lo and behold, it happened."

The hurt, the pain went away.

When Sparky spoke of Trammell being his clean-up hitter, all of baseball laughed. Trammell did, too. It was a crazy experiment. It was Sparky in the springtime.

JEFF SAMORAY ON ALAN TRAMMELL

I was always an Alan Trammell fan, and I'm lucky that I was able to watch him and Lou Whitaker snag hard grounders up the middle and turn double plays through their entire baseball careers.

From their scrawny, sunny rookie years to the twilight, that duo shined in smoothly making the difficult double plays. I'm sure they could have turned them in their sleep.

At first I liked both players equally, since they were conjoined both at second base and in the batting lineup. Even their statistics were near mirror images of each other. But Trammell separated himself, and became my all-time favorite player, in 1987.

With Lance Parrish gone, and in sore need of a cleanup hitter, Sparky Anderson made an almost unheard of move by inserting Trammell, a shortstop, in the prime power hitting slot. This was before shortstops like Derek Jeter and Nomar Garciaparra assumed their status as sluggers.

I don't think any fan could have foreseen that Trammell would respond to the challenge by a career year — hitting .343, with 28 home runs and 105 RBI — while leading Detroit to an American League East title. A MVP year if there ever was one. I'm still upset that he didn't win that award.

For all the double plays, my lasting memory of Trammell will be a grand slam he hit on a sweaty summer night in 1988. With the Tigers down by three runs with two outs in the bottom of the ninth, Trammell fouled off pitch after pitch on a full count before drilling a Cecilio Guante fastball to the upper deck for the game winner.

He was clutch — in the field and at the bat. In his prime, there wasn't a better shortstop in the league. There's certainly no other Tigers shortstop who can match Trammell's performance.

It was the smartest darn notion Sparky has had in his tinkering-laden career.

"It has happened," Trammell says of his leadership function. "I said years ago it's something I'd grow into. Respect

❖ ❖ ❖

Trammell is one of only three players to play 20 seasons in a Tigers uniform, joining Ty Cobb and Al Kaline.

has something to do with leadership. The younger guys look for me to do things. I can't afford to hit .230 and have 50 RBI. I have to do more for this club to win.

"I've got to be involved. Somehow."

For a season and a half, Trammell has hit baseballs with muscles he doesn't have. He has hit for high average. He has hit home runs. He has driven in runs. He has performed with brilliance in the field. And most vitally, his club finished first last year with an array of blue-collar role players. More amazingly, it is in first place again right now.

In the long range, the switch of Trammell to clean-up turned him into a potential Hall of Famer.

This ballclub soars on despite the defections of its stars Parrish and Kirk Gibson. It goes on, largely, because of Trammell and his involvement.

"I guess," he says, trying to figure this phenomenon, "it's because we're professionals."

◆ ◆ ◆

Shortstop: Alan Trammell 1977–96

He moved ahead of Billy Rogell on the all-time team because of his consistent play from 1977 to 1996. Who didn't respect this man, on and off the field? With Lou Whitaker, he formed the best double-play combination in Tigers history.

The more the Tigers asked of him, the more he delivered. After the Tigers lost Lance Parrish to free agency in 1987, they put Trammell into the cleanup position and he gave them his finest season—a .343 batting average, 28 homers and 105 RBI. He finished second to George Bell of Toronto for the MVP award.

He did win the MVP award in the 1984 World Series, playing with a confidence that rubbed off on the rest of his teammates. He never complained, never alibied and was courteous to all. Not bad for a guy who was nervous much of the time.

Trammell profile

World Series MVP in 1984. ... a six-time All-Star and a four-time Gold Glove winner. ... American League record holder with Lou Whitaker for most games played by teammates. ... Sixth in team history for runs and doubles, and seventh in hits and total bases. ... Best offensive year was 1987, when he hit .343 with 28 home runs, 105 RBI and 34 doubles. He is one of three players to play 20 seasons in a Tigers uniform, the others being Ty Cobb and Al Kaline. ... played 2,140 games at shortstop.

Alan Trammell's name can rarely be mentioned without including Lou Whitaker in the conversation.

Trammell jabs a thumb towards Sparky's office.

"When I retire, I'll miss the game," says Trammell. "I didn't want to do anything else."

There is this scenario. Sometime, perhaps a decade from now, George Anderson will elect to retire as manager in Detroit. His successor? Who could be better qualified? Who learned from the master? Who'd be more qualified to be the next manager of the Tigers than Alan Trammell, professional, Hall of Fame shortstop, table setter?

The dream is eternal.

❖ ❖ ❖

George
Kell

GEORGE KELL ✦ THIRD BASE ✦ 1946-1952

Kell was never a superstar, but he seemed like a Superman at third

By Joe Falls ✦ *The Detroit News*
ORIGINALLY PRINTED JULY 31, 1983

The days were different. People came downtown to catch a movie at the Michigan Theatre or the Madison or the United Artists and they might take their kids for a Chinese dinner at Victor Lim's. Or they might take them through Hudson's and show them all the wonders of the mighty department store.

If it got too hot, some would bring their blankets with them and spend the night on Belle Isle, searching for a breath of air.

This is how it was after the war — an age of innocence. The factories were running again, turning out peacetime products like those squat-looking cars with those wide running boards and radios that fit into the dashboard and could pick up Joe Gentile and Ralph Binge and their morning madness. Happy days were here again, and the ball club at Michigan and Trumbull played in bright sunshine and it was heartening to see High Henry back, along with Doc Cramer, Birdie Tebbetts and Dick Wakefield.

This is when George Kell, a bright-eyed, red-head-

ed young man, began playing third base for the Tigers. It was a good time because people felt good. The men were home from Remagen and Iwo Jima and Guadalcanal and it was time to get on with living. America after the war was returning to work, finding a house, buying a car, having babies.

Today, that bright-eyed, red-headed young man is 60 years old. He has not lost that twinkle in his eyes and at 2:30 p.m. he will be given the greatest honor of his life. George Kell will be enshrined in the Hall of Fame in Cooperstown, N.Y., along with Brooks Robinson, Juan Marichal and Walter Alston.

Kell batted .306 during a 15-year career, primarily with the Tigers. He also played with the Philadelphia Athletics,

✦ ✦ ✦

73

Jerry Green on George Kell

The 1949 American League season was memorable for an epic pennant race and a classic race for the batting championship. The Yankees beat the Red Sox by one game for the pennant. And the Tigers' George Kell nipped Ted Williams on the last day of the season to win the batting championship. Kell won by a fraction of a percentage point, batting .3429 to .3428.

Kell was baseball's top third baseman through the late 1940s and early 1950s. He batted over .300 in nine seasons, including in all seven in which he wore the Olde English D in Detroit. The Tigers got him during the 1946 season in a trade with the Philadelphia Athletics for Barney McCosky and dealt him to the Red Sox in an historic eight-player trade in 1952. He later played for the Orioles and White Sox, finishing with a career batting average of .306.

When his playing career ended, Kell returned to the Tigers as a play-by-play broadcaster in radio and television until his retirement after the 1996 season. Kell entered the Hall of Fame in 1983 and is one of only nine third basemen in Cooperstown.

Boston Red Sox, Chicago White Sox and Baltimore Orioles. Ironically, Kell closed his career in 1957 with Baltimore, where Robinson was beginning to earn his reputation as perhaps the slickest-fielding third baseman ever.

After years of being ignored in Hall of Fame voting, Kell was selected by the Committee of Veterans in March.

"When the phone rang that day, I knew I was in," said Kell, now a broadcaster on the Tigers' television network. "I have been in such a dream world since then. I'm sure that once I get on the grounds, it will hit me. Even now, when I think of being there with Babe Ruth and all the rest, I'm in awe."

Today is a day George Kell has long dreamed about . . . ever since bumping into Connie Mack in the elevator of the Sheraton-Cadillac Hotel in May of 1946.

The venerable Mr. Mack had been out to the ball park and they told him that a new elevator had been installed to the front office and wondered if he would like to take a ride in it. "Why not?" he said, and he rode it to the third floor. That's where the general manager of the Tigers — George Trautman — had his office.

Mack walked in and before any pleasantries could be exchanged, he said to Trautman: "How would you like to have a third baseman?"

Mr. Mack was talking about his bright-eyed, red-headed third baseman who had not performed in the manner expected of him by the Philadelphia patriarch.

Trautman, of course, was interested. Third base was a trouble spot for the Tigers. They hadn't had a solid third baseman since Pinky Higgins, and when Mr. Mack said, "I will trade you Mr. Kell for one of your outfielders," Trautman scratched out the names of five outfielders and gave Mack his choice. He picked Barney McCosky, and the two men shook hands. It was a straight man-for-man deal.

Now, back at the hotel, there was some consternation among players on the Philadelphia club. The Athletics were to fly to St. Louis after the game, and air travel was not the accepted mode of travel in those days. They lived on trains. Mr. Mack put it up to a vote of the players and when he met Kell on the elevator, he said: "George, you are staying here today."

"Oh, no, Mr. Mack," answered Kell, "I voted in favor of flying. I'll go with you."

"I'm afraid not," said Mack. "You'll stay here. I just traded you for Barney McCosky."

The bright-eyed, red-headed young third baseman stayed in Detroit for almost seven seasons and grew into one of the premier players in the game. He played in the time of Joe DiMaggio and Ted Williams and excelled in a way that earned him the respect of players, managers, fans and members of the media.

He was not a super star in the sense of DiMaggio or Williams. But he has a kind of a flair of his own that commanded the attention of anyone who saw him play. It could be called intensity, mixed with intelligence.

❖ ❖ ❖

George Kell worked hard in seven seasons with the Tigers, batting under .300 only once.

The game wasn't easy for him. He had to work for everything. He was slow of foot but displayed a determination that drew the admiration of those around him. George Kell came to play.

He went at the game with the same curiosity that he did as a history teacher back in his home of Swifton, Ark. He wanted to know everything that was going on.

Hours before the game, he'd be out there examining the ground around third base. He wanted to see if it was hard or soft, wet or dry. He'd check the wind conditions, the intensity of the sun and anything else that would give him an edge. He always had a serious look on his face and that gave people the wrong impression of him.

If you saw him in the batting cage, you saw a man with

❖ ❖ ❖

75

Kell won a batting title in 1949.

a desire on his face that was almost frightening. He had thoughts of one thing and one thing only: that white ball which was bearing down on him from the pitching

Third base: George Kell 1946-1952

Became first third baseman in American League history to win a batting title in 1949. He beat out Ted Williams .3429 to .3427 and he did it on the final day of the season, getting two hits while the Boston slugger went hitless.

GEORGE CLYDE KELL
PHILADELPHIA A. L. 1943-1946
DETROIT A. L. 1946-1952
BOSTON A. L. 1952-1954
CHICAGO A. L. 1954-1956
BALTIMORE A. L. 1956-1957
PREMIER A. L. THIRD BASEMAN OF 1940'S AND
1950'S. SOLID HITTER AND SURE-HANDED FIELDER
WITH STRONG, ACCURATE ARM. BATTED OVER
.300 9 TIMES, LEADING LEAGUE WITH .343 IN
1949. LED A. L. THIRD BASEMEN IN FIELDING
PCT. 7 TIMES, ASSISTS 4 TIMES AND PUTOUTS
AND DOUBLE PLAYS TWICE.

Kell was no cheese champion and came right back and hit .340 the following season. Kell played seven seasons in Detroit and was a consistent .300 hitter. And for seven years he was named the league's leading third baseman.

One of his most memorable moments came the day Joe DiMaggio smashed a hard grounder off his face, breaking Kell's jaw, but he got up from the ground and threw out the Yankee star at first base.

Kell profile

Inducted into the Hall of Fame in 1983, becoming one of eight third basemen to be enshrined. ... Beat out Boston's Ted Williams to win 1949 batting crown with a .343 average. ... Named to All-Star team in six of seven seasons with the Tigers, and eight consecutive overall. ... Included in eight-player trade with Boston in 1952, going to the Red Sox along with Dizzy Trout, Hoot Evers and Johnny Lipon for Johnny Pesky, Walt Dropo, Bill Wight, Fred Hatfield and Don Lenhardt.

mound. He was not one of the merry makers. No drinking, no carousing. His mind was set only on that white ball.

Nobody ever made a greater study of hitting than George Kell. He applied himself in ways that others could not understand. He spoke to everybody he could about hitting, players, manager, umpires and even the old scouts who would sit up in the stands and watch the pregame workouts.

It was nothing for him to change his stance between pitches — moving back for fastballs, up for curves —

❖ ❖ ❖

and trying for every percentage available to him. Lyall Smith, who wrote about Kell in his finest days, said it was nothing for Kell to assume as many as four different stances in one turn at bat.

The result was a consistency that made Kell the outstanding third baseman of his day. Nine times he batted .300. He won the batting title with a .343 mark in 1949–the first third baseman in American League history to perform the feat.

His favorite base hit — the one he seemed to invent — was the line double into the left field corner. His two-base hits became a part of the lore and legend of the game: "Kell takes his stance, leaning over, here's the pitch — there's a shot down the left field line, it's into the corner..."

He hit 56 of them one season and drove the poor pitchers to distraction. In the field, Kell displayed even more intensity with the glove than he did with the bat. He was ready on every play, rising up on his toes and jumping into position as if daring the batter to hit one his way. In his day, nobody was better in the field.

They never gave him a nickname because he wasn't a nickname type of player.

He simply came out each day and gave them a professional performance, and how nice it would be when the Tigers honor him next summer, if they will let him go to the plate one more time and throw him enough pitches until he lines one into the left field corner, two hops off the wall, for a double.

Kell (in 1951 photo) was a magician at third base.

George Kell's statistical career

Year	AB	R	H	HR	RBI	Avg.
1946	434	67	142	4	41	.327
1947	588	75	188	5	93	.206
1948	368	47	112	2	44	.304
1949	522	97	179	3	59	.343
1950	541	114	218	8	101	.340
1951	598	92	191	2	59	.319
1952	152	11	45	1	17	.296

❖ ❖ ❖

77

Bill
Freehan

Bill Freehan ✦ Catcher ✦ 1961, 1963-1976

Freehan, a rock behind the plate, took the position to new heights

By Jerry Green ✦ *The Detroit News*
Originally printed August 9, 1988

At 3:06, St. Louis time, on the afternoon of Oct. 10. 1968, Bill Freehan caught Tim McCarver's pop foul to the right of the plate. In an instant, Mickey Lolich jumped into Freehan's arms. An entire ballclub pounded atop the two of them.

Back in Detroit, people came out of the office buildings and kissed and yelled and honked their horns. Paper fluttered from the windows and piled up calf-deep, and the people had trouble walking through it. And there was so much confetti thrown, it lined the embankments of the expressways for 15 miles from downtown.

"My back's never been the same since," Freehan said in a flashback to that day 20 years ago.

The Tigers had won the World Series — in their normal suspense-story style.

The pop foul, swirling up and then spinning back down, is perhaps the toughest play for the catcher.

"I knew it was not a difficult play," Freehan said. "The only thing concerning me was that Norm Cash and I — because Norman was very good at pop-ups —

Bill Freehan's 1,581 games behind the plate remains the standard for Tigers catchers.

✦ ✦ ✦

didn't run together.

"You're this close to the championship. Make sure you do everything technically right. Now the world rides on you making just that mechanical action."

Freehan had all the poise he needed.

"It's an instant," Freehan said. "It flashes through your mind, like, 'Norman, Norman, I got it, don't run into me,' and just watching the ball right into your glove. I can recall it vividly — I'm not hitting very well.

"The least I could do is catch the last out."

Freehan had played with poise all season. He offered a quiet, unemotional leadership to a team that played with wild, bizarre emotions. He caught Denny McLain and Lolich and the sulking Joe Sparma. He played with an even flow — the counterbalance to the highs and lows of Cash, Jim Northrup, Gates Brown, Willie Horton. He provided right-handed punch while Al Kaline mended on the disabled list.

In the World Series, he suffered through a tortuous batting slump, starting 1-for-18, ultimately 2-for-24 for the Series — .083.

"You can be philosophical about it," Freehan said. "How many times during the season do you go 1-for-18? Probably three or four times. Except you don't have 80 million people watching you."

But Freehan's staunch catching was vital for the Tigers. He caught the last out. And he blocked the plate on the play which turned the world Series around—from a rout by the Cardinals to a seven-game comeback drama for the Tigers. Still, today, Freehan is certain that he tagged Lou Brock out at the plate in Game 5. Brock is just as certain that he was safe, that he beat Horton's throw from left.

"I positioned myself," Freehan said. "That's the technical way we are all taught to block at plate. Then, without a good throw you can't block the plate. Horton made a heckuva throw. It was about waist high. And had Lou slid, I don't know. We've hashed this thing around a million times since then.

GEORGE CANTOR ON BILL FREEHAN

The moment is frozen in memory. Lou Brock streaks towards the plate, needing just one more step to cross and give St. Louis the run it needs to turn back the Tigers' last challenge of the 1968 World Series.

His foot descends, but in the fractional second before it can make contact it is blocked and deflected by the left hip of Bill Freehan. Brock is spun aside and Freehan whirls with the ball to tag him out.

The entire Series whirled with him. Although he had been held hitless until that point, Freehan's block ended St. Louis' chance to put the Tigers away. From that instant on, it was all Detroit.

It was a football player's block, and that is what Freehan had been, an end at the University of Michigan, before joining the Tigers.

He was a raw talent, at first; a big, strong kid whose natural ability was enough to get him into the lineup on a young ballclub. But he learned fast, and within a few seasons was able to call the game for some of the quirkiest, strangest and most talented pitchers in the team's history.

Freehan was a thoughtful athlete who worked hard to get better. But so much of his energy was put into improving the mental part of his game, the ability to think along with his pitcher and outsmart the opposition, that he never became a consistently dominant hitter. His throwing arm was always a bit suspect, too.

But his durability, intelligence and sheer determination to master the most demanding position on the field, made Freehan the game's outstanding catcher of the 1960s.

He won his position on the all-time Tigers team the old fashioned way: He earned it.

"Every time I see him, he says he thinks I never touched him, and I say 'I don't think you ever touched home plate. And he says, 'Why'd you come after me and tag me a second time if you thought you tagged me the first time?' I said, 'If you look at the replay after the collision he spins away and he starts running back to touch home plate. I say,' 'If you thought you touched

Freehan's career as a football player helped when he had to stand his ground at the plate.

home plate the first time, why'd you come back?'

"Everybody looks back and says it was a turning point in the Series, but at that time you had no idea that's going to happen. You just try to make a play. Without a good throw from Horton and maybe a little indecision on Brock's part, who knows?"

Freehan caught most of McLain's 31 victories.

"I remember the crazy coming-from-behind situations," said Freehan. "The magic season he had. Catching a lot of it. You look at how easy he won so many games.

The crazy things he did. Crazy to an outside person, but it was indicative of his personality. And of all the pitchers I caught, I don't think he ever, ever, ever lost confidence in his own ability, I mean supreme confidence.

"You'd come out to the mound and he'd say, 'What are you coming out here for? You're just wasting time. Get on back in there. I'll think of something.'

"And then Boog Powell would hit a line drive right back at him and it would be a triple play and he's out of the inning."

◆ ◆ ◆

Freehan a hit before his Tigers debut

By Doc Green ✦ *The Detroit News*
ORIGINALLY PRINTED FEBRUARY 18, 1962

Bill Freehan's statistical career

Year	AB	R	H	HR	RBI	Avg.
1961	10	1	4	0	4	.400
1963	300	37	73	9	36	.243
1964	520	69	156	18	80	.300
1965	431	45	101	10	43	.234
1966	492	47	115	12	46	.234
1967	517	66	146	20	74	.282
1968	540	73	142	25	84	.263
1969	489	61	128	16	49	.262
1970	395	44	95	16	52	.241
1971	516	57	143	21	71	.277
1972	374	51	98	10	56	.262
1973	380	33	89	6	29	.234
1974	445	58	132	18	60	.297
1975	427	42	105	14	47	.246
1976	237	22	64	5	27	.270

In the bullpen at Henley Field, the pitchers were waiting their turn to pitch the one inning in the first intrasquad game of the early camp when this large animal approached the batter's box.

"Here's the phenom now," remarked Hank Aguirre casually and without rancor. "Maybe the best looking rookie I ever saw."

Bill Freehan — the Detroit $100,000 gamble — selected a pitch and lined it off the left-field wall for two bases.

"Easy, ain't it," said Aguirre.

The 20-year-old Detroit catching property singled his next time at bat, did all the things he was supposed to do as a backstop, then was extracted from the line-up and trotted out to the bullpen to help warm up the impending pitchers.

Neither General Manager Rick Ferrell nor Manager Bob Scheffing, both of them ex-catchers, expect the Royal Oak stripling of 6 feet 3, 218 pounds to suddenly alleviate the hoary problem that exists behind the plate for the Tigers.

"On the other hand," remarked Ferrell, "you sort of keep waiting for him to do something wrong."

Freehan sat down on a folding chair and wiped the perspiration from the high cheekbones derived from the trace of Indian blood on his maternal side.

"Have I thought about making it the first year?" he answered. "I guess yes. I think about it. But I'm not catching well. I made a lot of mistakes last year at Duluth and Knoxville. It was embarrassing. I made mistakes I know better than to make. I had a lot of passed balls."

He's sort of a half-bashful young man, friendly, unassuming and popular with the other players, a kid who has beaten the jealousy rap through a natural modesty.

"I don't worry about hitting any," he said blithely. "But, well, I like to the run the game. That's one of the reasons I like catching. But it's hard for a kid like me to call pitchers for (Don) Mossi or (Frank) Lary or anybody, for that matter. That would be tough."

Since if he doesn't worry about hitting, he's the only ball player in the history of this summer nonsense who doesn't, this seemed to merit further explanation.

> *"I would like to be the best catcher that, well, there's ever been. Isn't that something. I've got a long way to go."*
>
> BILL FREEHAN

✦ ✦ ✦

Catcher: Bill Freehan 1961, 1963-76

A product of the Detroit sandlots and the Unversity of Michigan, from 1963 to 1976, with a brief appearance in 1961. He called the pitches for the 1968 champions but even more impressive is that he played for eight managers and they all wanted him to catch their way.

This meant he had to make constant adjustments in his style, not to mention his thinking. It was like he had to keep relearning the game to suit his bosses. He never complained, never used it as an alibi when things weren't going well.

He was a rock behind the plate — a large man who knew what he was doing. He was not a great hitter but he was dependable in everything he did — a complete team player.

Freehan's profile

An 11-time All-Star, the Detroit native spent his entire career with the Tigers. ... Won five Gold Gloves during his 15-year career. ... Has the third highest fielding percentage (.993) among catchers. ... Played in 11 All-Star games, including 10 in a row. He caught all 15 innings of the 1967 All-Star game. Ninth in team history in home runs, and 10th in games played.

"I've just always hit," he said simply.

Always, means from back in the sixth and seventh grades when the Tiger talent searcher Louis d'Annunzio first began to hear reports about him. He continued to "always hit" summers on the local sandlots when he was playing for Vince Desmond, and at 2 o'clock in the morning last spring, the night the NCAA college baseball tournament in Omaha was over and he became eligible and did sign a contract, he'd still always hit.

He'd set a new Big Ten hitting record of .434 at Michigan to break a mark established by Yankee first baseman Bill Skowron, when the latter was battling the professors at Purdue.

Last season Freehan played his first professional bit at Duluth, opening there in a doubleheader and getting four hits while stirring the citizenry with his throws to second base.

Between games they placed a small nail keg on second base for one of those turns of hippodrome employed in the minors, and Freehan knocked the keg off the bag with his first two throws.

He graduated from Duluth to Knoxville and then in the final two weeks of the season to Detroit where, as you know, he hit .400 in his first testing at major league pitching. What had he said? "Always hit."

"I'm not catching well though," he said again.

"Did you ever consider playing somewhere else?," seemed a proper question.

"Absolutely not," he said, making it sound like a declaration. "I've played the outfield and first base, but what's the quickest way up to the big leagues? Catching. Suppose I was an outfielder, I've got (Al) Kaline, (Billy) Bruton and (Rocky) Colavito in front of me. I could get old waiting. Or at first base — I'd have (Norm) Cash. No, I'm a catcher."

He paused a moment.

"I would like to be the best catcher that, well, there's ever been. Isn't that something. I've got a long way to go."

Later, Ferrell mentioned, "You know, after the game I said something like 'nice going' to him and he said that to me about how he wasn't catching well. He's catching better than he thinks he is. He's big for a catcher but he gets down low and he's in perfect balance. A catcher has trouble with low balls in the dirt but they don't seem to bother him too much."

"He's the first guy out in the morning and the last one in," offered business manager Jimmy Campbell. "You have to keep him from wearing himself out."

As I said, no one seriously thinks that Freehan will make it his first year — since no one ever does — but they watch and wait.

They're waiting for him to do something wrong.

And holding their breath that he won't.

Jack
Morris

JACK MORRIS ✦ RIGHT HAND PITCHER ✦ 1977-1990

Mt. Morris could explode at any moment, but so could his fastball

By Joe Falls ✦ *The Detroit News*
ORIGINALLY PRINTED FEBRUARY 6, 1991

If I had to sum up Jack Morris in one word, the word would be: Mad. He always seemed to be mad at something. Or somebody. And he let his anger show. He made little effort to hide it. He was always seething. He was at his worst when he was sneering at people.

I never understood him. Not fully anyway. I knew he was a great competitor.

You have to give the man that much. He would get mad when things didn't go right. He could get upset with himself, his fielders, his batters — even his manager — and it would just tear him up. He could not retain his composure.

He had to lash out at somebody.

Usually it was members of the media.

Morris could hardly take it out on his teammates, except in oblique ways. He had to live with them and work with them. He would rip management for not doing the things he thought they should do to have a better

Jack Morris is a smart guy, but not as smart as he thinks he is. If he was, he wouldn't have had all this trouble in Detroit ... and he would have been a much happier man.

team. Again, he seldom named names.

Morris' favorite target became the media — mostly the writers. He lashed out at them again and again, and if you didn't hear the anger in his voice, you could see it in his face.

He never cared for us that much. I always felt he thought we were a little on the stupid side. What he really felt, in my opinion, is that he couldn't control us, and that was a source of irritation to him.

Morris — a strong pitcher — could be the ultimate enigma. A couple of years ago he sounded off to a couple of Minnesota writers about the way the Tigers were doing something. Or not doing something. The subject is not important.

✦ ✦ ✦

85

He told the Minnesota writers not to tell the Detroit writers how he felt, but they did the moment they got to the press box. That was wrong of the Minnesota writers. They should have kept their word to Morris.

But the Detroit writers were going to find out the next morning when they read the Minneapolis and St. Paul papers. Morris' blast was top-line stuff.

So, what did Morris do when he found out the Minnesota writers spilled the beans to the Detroit writers? Did he get mad at them? Nope. He got mad at the Detroit writers and wouldn't speak to them for the rest of the season.

I always felt bad that Morris had such a chip on his shoulder because he knew more about the workings of baseball than anyone on the team, and he had the ability to express himself in ways that nobody else did. He had the best mind, I thought, since Al Kaline.

I liked talking baseball with him because he was so well versed. We would have this one good discussion every spring. It would take place in the first week of camp. I'd try to go to him with thoughtful questions, and he always responded with some wonderful answers.

But that was it.

Before long somebody would write something he didn't like — and it usually wasn't me, though I took my shots — and he wouldn't talk anymore. I felt a lot of wisdom went to waste.

One year I talked him into doing a five-part series on how to pitch in the major leagues. To this day, I felt it was some of the best baseball writing I have ever done, not because of my efforts ... I merely recorded his words ... but because of all the revealing things he had to say about himself and his profession.

George Will, the national columnist from Washington, was so impressed with Morris' comments that he called me and said he was doing a book on baseball and wanted Morris to be the subject of his

TOM GAGE ON JACK MORRIS

Sometimes Jack Morris was too competitive for his own good. It gave him an angry edge. But that edge was just another reason Morris became an outstanding pitcher.

As a reporter, it took me a long time to figure Jack out. Maybe I never did. But at least I think I did. On a different level, verbal instead of physical, we were his opposition almost as much as the hitters in the box.

The competition didn't stop with the final out for Morris, now it was time to compete with the media after the game. What he expected, however, and what he liked most was for us to be as competitive with him as he was with us. Jack wanted repartee, he thrived on challenging responses. That was his nature.

I remember flying back to Detroit from Boston years ago. It wasn't the team flight, but for some reason Morris was on it. He and the media were at odds at the time, one of those occasions, so you imagine how we both felt when we found that we were sitting next to each other on the flight.

But instead of silence in this forced environment, we ended up talking the entire way on a variety of subjects.

No baseball, though.

It was a turning point for me in understanding him. At the ballparks, he had opponents. He wanted opponents. Off the field, though, we weren't a threat.

It was all a game, a marvelous challenge game to Jack Morris. He was good at it. One of the best.

section on pitching.

I told him all I knew about Jack and sent him some day newspaper clips from our files.

When the book came out, Will wrote about Orel Hershiser of the Los Angeles Dodgers. I asked him what happened to Morris and Will said: "He just wouldn't cooperate with me."

Jack Morris is a smart guy, but not as smart as he thinks he is. If he was, he wouldn't have had all this trouble in Detroit ... and he would have been a much happier man.

♦ ♦ ♦

Durable Morris pitched through the pain

By Doug Bradford
Originally printed May 29, 1978

Jack Morris turned back the clock Saturday. Time will tell if the 22-year-old Tiger right-hander made the right gamble.

"Just give me the ball," Morris said during the week. "I don't care if my shoulder hurts. I'll pitch anyway."

Ah, the words to gladden the hearts of those who remember the one-cent Babe Ruth candy bar, 10-cent movies, three-cent stamps, Ty Cobb's slashing spikes...

Now *there*'s a pitcher, the old-timers say, that Morris.

Why everyone knows that pitching arms hurt; that you just got to grit your teeth and hum it. Whoever heard of Bob Feller or Lefty Grove or Walter Johnson having tendinitis?

Whoever heard of phlebitis until President Nixon had it?

There is, you see, a growing suspicion among some that Mark "The Bird" Fidrych and Dave "The Rose" Rozema have a bigger problem in their heads than in their shoulders. Like one is attached to the other.

Rozema and Fidrych are on the zany side, say the oldsters. Maybe they just *think* their shoulders hurt.

They sure are thinking about them, Fidrych went into such a funk before being sent to Florida for treatment under the sun that he wouldn't talk — not even to the baseball.

Rozema said yesterday he is going to consult his private doctor to find out why he can't pitch

Morris won 20 games twice with the Tigers.

◆ ◆ ◆

87

more than a few innings without pain.

He showed the palms of his hands, which were shedding skin.

"Nerves," he said.

Morris doesn't know what's wrong with his shoulder, and maybe his problem isn't as severe as those of his teammates.

But he's sure he has the pain. It found him last July and it hasn't left since.

Morris had gone only 3⅔ innings on May 18, against Milwaukee before the pain drove him to the bench.

Then he was rocked in one inning of relief on May 21 against Boston. The Tigers called up Steve Baker from the minors and dispatched Morris to relief duty.

Demoted to the bullpen to find new strength, Morris became anxious to work back into the starting rotation.

So Morris said to hell with the pain, and went after the Red Sox in three good innings Saturday in relief. He made one bad pitch — a changeup — and Jim Rice popped it over the short left-field wall.

"One of those soft ones," said old-timers. "Boy, you got to fire that rock."

Dizzy Dean used to call it "Powder River." Today, it's good velocity. Well, times have changed.

No matter. It will be interesting to see if Morris can fight his way back and live up to the promise of his 1977 showing.

"I can't rear back now," he said, "so I have to put my body more into it, and I came through with my arm different. I can't muscle the ball up there."

He went through a series of motions to demonstrate. If he can't pitch he might make a good third base coach.

Some pitchers live with tendinitis, others cannot. One who does is Boston's Bill Lee.

Morris transformed his anger into 198 victories.

Jack Morris's statistical career

Year	W-L	IP	H	HR	SO	ERA
1977	1-1	45	38	4	28	3.74
1978	3-5	106	107	8	48	4.33
1979	17-7	197	179	19	113	3.28
1980	16-15	250	252	20	112	4.18
1981	14-7	198	153	14	97	3.05
1982	17-16	266	247	37	135	4.06
1983	20-13	293	257	30	232	3.34
1984	18-11	240	221	20	148	3.60
1985	16-11	257	212	21	191	3.33
1986	21-8	267	229	40	223	3.27
1987	18-11	266	227	39	208	3.38
1988	15-13	235	225	20	168	3.94
1989	6-14	170	189	23	115	4.86
1990	15-18	249	231	26	162	4.51

◆ ◆ ◆

Right-handed pitcher:
Jack Morris 1977-1990

They called him Mt. Morris because of his volcanic explosions on the field and in the clubhouse. He would often apologize for his behavior, then get mad again.

He was a tremendous competitor, Sparky Anderson's most dependable pitcher. He brought the split-finger pitch to a high level. It helped him to two 20-game seasons and a no-hitter.

And he liked to talk the tough talk. He said: "I like to embarrass players on other teams. I like making them look bad because that's what they're trying to do to me."

But he could also be the imp. When he was asked for an interview before a big series with Toronto, he said: "Hi everybody!

"This is the biggest series in the history of baseball. If we lose, we are finished for all time. If we win, we are World Champions.

"Thank you and goodbye."

Morris' profile

In 14 seasons with the Tigers, Morris was the team's dominant pitcher. ... During the 1980s he averaged 16 victories each season. During the decade his 162 victories, 133 complete games, 2,443 innings and 332 starts was tops in baseball. His 1,629 strikeouts were third behind only Nolan Ryan and Fernando Valenzuela. ... Named to four All-Star games, and started in 1981 and 1985. ... Won 20 games twice. ... Tossed a no-hitter at Comiskey Park on April 7, 1984.

Morris averaged 16 wins a year during the 1980s.

He has his own theory, claiming that a lack of oxygen in the stomach is the culprit.

If you have a tough stomach, he says, you won't have a bad shoulder.

A guy out in California claims that the physical ailments that plague today's young ballplayers stem from nutritional deficiency.

Of course, he sells nutrients with scientific names. In the old days they would have called him a medicine man and his wares elixir or snake oil.

✦ ✦ ✦

Hal
Newhouser

Hal Newhouser ✦ Left-Hand Pitcher ✦ 1939-1953

Newhouser dominated his era, but 'wartime player' label lingered

By Lynn Henning ✦ *The Detroit News*
Originally printed June 3, 1986

At a dusty ballyard in Detroit, or at one of those neat, cyclone-fenced suburban parks where the grass actually features more sod than weeds, Hal Newhouser sometimes spots a good one.

He will be 6-foot-2 or 6-3, run well, throw well, swing a good bat, too, even if he's a pitching prospect. He will be an athlete. A raw talent. The kind of kid Newhouser and the Houston Astros club for which he scouts may want to sign.

Newhouser will study something else as he sits inconspicuously in the stands.

He will look for clues as to the youngster's psychological makeup. Is the kid serious about baseball? Serious enough to study the game and develop some elementary form of a pitching stratagem?

There will be clues as Newhouser inspects from his cold bleacher seat. And if the salt-and-pepper-haired scout detects that the kid has a bit of a temper to go with his teen-age prowess, Newhouser's interest climbs, because that was precisely his style during a 15-year career in Detroit that somehow escaped being a Hall of Fame career. (Newhouser was finally inducted

William G. Evans and Newhouser hold a lucky horseshoe as Newhouser signs his contract in 1948.

in 1992).

His temper, concedes Hal Newhouser, exceeded anything shown by modern-day Tigers smokestack Jack Morris. "Mine was 10 times worse than his,"

✦ ✦ ✦

Newhouser says, munching on a club sandwich. "Ever been in the tunnel leading from the dugout to club-house?

"Yeah. Light bulbs. They could always count how far I was through — pow-pow-pow — I took every one of em. Somebody would say, 'Oh, Hal's up the steps now.'

"There were a few buttons off the uniform, too."

He broke in with Detroit in 1939, went to Cleveland in 1954, and was out of baseball the following year, taking with him some monstrous numbers: 207 victories, 150 defeats, a 3.06 earned run average and back-to-back Most Valuable Player awards in 1944 and 45 — the only major-leaguer ever to win consecutive MVP titles.

He destroyed the league from 1944-46, rolling up records of 29-9, 25-9 and 26-9. The ERA numbers were equally overwhelming: 2.22, 1.81 and 1.94.

And then there were the classic Sunday duels that baseball historians still cite as some of the game's finest hours in pure head-to-head pitching artistry: Newhouser vs. Cleveland's Bob Feller. Plan on a 1-0, 2-1 game. And about an hour, 45 minutes would do it.

"It never was preprogrammed," explains Newhouser, who turned 65 last month.

"In those days, you played four games each series, and each team went into a town four times. We worked Opening Day, so our matchup was it from the start. I knew and he knew we were gonna have a battle."

An understatement there.

Feller would walk to the mound ready to throw a breathtaking inning of pure lightning bolts. His fastball was unmatched, and his curveball — the pitch was virtually unhittable it broke so viciously — is still mentioned in the same God-fearing tones normally reserved for natural disasters.

Newhouser wasn't as powerful, but he had all the pitches, and above all, he had control. Often that was

Jerry Green on Hal Newhouser

In 1940, Hal Newhouser was in high school in Detroit, learning manual arts. Unlike his classmates, who earned spending money as soda jerks or busboys, Newhouser was a rookie major-league pitcher with the Tigers.

The Tigers played only day games back then at Briggs Stadium. And when classes were out, the Newhouser, still a teenager, would hustle to the streetcar in time for the 3:30 ballgame.

Young lefty Hal went 9-9 that rookie season, displaying a streak of wildness and a wild temper. In the seasons to come, as he became a veteran, he curbed both. He would have seasons of 29, 25, 26, 17, 21 18 and 15 victories in succession, the premier lefthander in the major leagues during the 1940s. In '45, he pitched the Tigers to a seven-game victory over the Cubs in the World Series. He was twice voted the most valuable player in the American League.

Called a "wartime pitcher" by skeptics, Newhouser proved his critics wrong after World War II ended. Ted Williams called Newhouser one of the three toughest pitchers he ever faced.

Newhouser pitched for the Tigers in 15 seasons and two more for Cleveland. He was elected to the Hall of Fame in 1992, six years before his death.

the difference: Feller might walk four batters in an inning for a run, or put a couple on and give up one of the two or three singles he would ration for the day.

Newhouser only hoped he could take a lead into the late innings. Then, the mind game started. It's why he pays such attention to mental tendencies in today's pitchers.

Against Feller, the thinking started early.

"I would train a little different because I would look so forward to the game," he explains. "I would do more calisthenics, more running, more thinking about their hitters. I tried to fine-tune myself a little more than against other pitchers.

♦ ♦ ♦

"You see, I pitched a little different. I had a philosophy that I pitched against the pitcher and I did not pitch against the hitters. The vast percentage of the time the ball was in my hand, everything was in my favor. I had to figure against Feller we were only gonna beat 'em by one run, so if I'm not ahead, I'm gone in the seventh inning for a pinch hitter. That was my philosophy: Stay on top. Stay on top. Stay on top."

There was another slogan popular during Newhouser's dominating days in Detroit: "I Want You." Uncle Sam was calling all the able-bodied to help in a war effort, and that included baseball players.

It also would have included Hal Newhouser if he had his druthers. He didn't.

After enlisting in the Air Corps, and passing his written exam, doctors informed him a heart murmur would rule him out as a pilot. Next stop was the Navy Air Corps, which told him the same thing.

Then the Army, where infantryman duty suggested a less picky physical. Again 4-F.

Newhouser was left to join other military rejects in a watered-down game.

"Wartime player" has since been equivalent to wearing an asterisk on one's forehead. It branded players as inferior participants in a then-inferior sport.

He sits in a restaurant booth, lightly tanned from watching ball games and playing golf, and Newhouser smiles at the "wartime" stigma. He can somewhat understand why his 54 victories from 1944-45 were pooh-poohed, but wonders why his 26-9 effort in 46, when the boys were back, isn't acknowledged. Or the 21-12 in 48.

The Newhouser saga began early in Detroit. He was born near the old Olympia, but his father, a wood pattern-maker, later moved the family to the Livernois-Fenkell area of town. Hal was a sandlot star back when amateur baseball was at its peak in Detroit, and it was no shock when he and the Tigers agreed to a contract not long after he left Wilbur Wright Trade School

Left-handed pitcher: Hal Newhouser 1939-1953

A stylist — a long and lanky Hall of Famer. The classic southpaw. A fierce competitor with a nasty temperment. His duels with Bob Feller were legend. The Tigers and Cleveland Indians would save their two stars to pitch against each other and fill their ballparks. Each respected the other and despite their great rivalry, they became friends in later years.

Some critics questioned Newhouser's credentials when he won 29 and 25 during World War II. He won consecutive MVP awards but they felt he did it against second-rate competition. His answer: He posted a 26-9 record in 1946 and 21-12 in 1948.

Newhouser's profile

Inducted into the Hall of Fame in 1992. ... The Detroit native is the only pitcher to win back-to-back MVP awards (1944-45). ... Finished 29-9 in 1944, and in 1945 became the third pitcher to lead the majors in victories (25), strikeouts (212) and ERA (1.81) in the same season. ... was a seven-time All-Star in 17 major-league seasons. ... Third in club history in strikeouts and fourth in in victories, shutouts and complete games. ... Tigers retired his number (16) in 1997.

(now Murray-Wright High).

He got married — he and his wife, Beryl, are going on 45 years — had two daughters, and got on with the business of torturing American League batters until one night in 1948.

"I had pitched a night game and got knocked out in the third inning," Newhouser recalls. "On the way home with my wife, I had my arm on the window ledge for about 15 minutes, and when I took it down, it was completely numb."

By the next year, it was agonizing.

"I mean it hurt," he remembers. "There was no muscle soreness, but it was so deep in the joint. Even today, if the kids come around to play ball, as soon as the ball leaves my fingertips, it feels like hot spikes being driven into the joint."

He believes, too, the pain kept him from winning 300 games.

Newhouser was only 28 when the arm began trou-

Newhouser led the league in wins, strikeouts and ERA in 1945.

bling him, and he was out of baseball at 33. That, too, has hurt his Cooperstown stock as much as World War II.

But dispense with any sympathy, he insists. He and Beryl live comfortably in Bloomfield Hills because of what baseball has done for Hal Newhouser. He went on to a successful 20-year career with Community National Bank (now First of America) because of his baseball identity.

And, he now scouts the youngsters and spends his retirement days doing what he always loved doing best: lapping up a game that has brought him such comfort and joy.

"This is the twilight of my life," he says, sipping an iced tea. "I'm so happy and so satisfied with what I'm doing. It's a delightful way to bow out."

Only one thing could make it more delightful, induction into the Hall of Fame.

"It's gonna happen, it's gonna happen," he says, his famed left arm thrusting.

"I may not be here. But sooner or later, maybe next year, maybe 10 or 20 years from now, it will happen. It has to happen.

"The only thing," says Hal Newhouser, his voice ringing. "I would like to be alive and well enough to accept it if it ever does happen. I have a lot of hope."

◆ ◆ ◆

Newhouser's wait for Hall nearly over

By George Cantor ✦ *The Detroit News*
ORIGINALLY PRINTED JULY 29, 1992

Hal Newhouser's statistical career

Year	W-L	IP	H	HR	SO	ERA
1939	0-1	5	3	0	4	5.40
1940	9-9	133	149	12	89	4.86
1941	9-11	173	166	6	106	4.79
1942	8-14	183	137	4	103	2.45
1943	8-17	195	163	3	144	3.04
1944	29-9	312	264	6	187	2.22
1945	25-9	313	239	5	212	1.81
1946	26-9	292	215	10	275	1.94
1947	17-17	285	268	9	176	2.87
1948	21-12	272	249	10	143	3.01
1949	18-11	292	277	19	144	3.36
1950	15-13	213	232	23	87	4.34
1951	6-6	96	98	10	37	3.92
1952	9-9	154	148	13	57	3.74
1953	0-1	21	31	4	6	7.06

It is springtime in Detroit, 1946. The war has been won, the boys are home, the air is alive with the possibilities of the good life that is coming.

To make it even better, the Tigers are defending World Champions, the Indians are in town and Briggs Stadium is rocking with the first of what will become legendary duels.

Bob Feller, out of the Navy, is striking out people at a record pace.

And facing him is Detroit's own Hal Newhouser, the left-hander from Livernois and Fenkell, who became the best pitcher in baseball during the war.

There it is.

"You'll use the phrase," he said, as we sat over lunch in Birmingham, a few days before he will fly to Cooperstown and be inducted into Baseball's Hall of Fame.

"You won't be able to help it. They hang a label on you, and that's the way it is. They call you Prince Hal, and that's nice. But then they also add 'wartime player,' and that's the one that sticks."

The war is finally over for Newhouser. After 46 years, the questions and the doubts and the anger have finally dissolved. Now, at age 71, he takes his rightful place with the game's elite, the best pitchers who ever took the mound. No one can dare use that label again.

"When I look back at my career, 1946 was the critical year," He says. "They were saying it even back then, you know. Even though I'd won 54 games in two years, plus two in the World Series, plus two Most Valuable Player awards, plus the pitching Triple Crown — that's what they were saying, 'wartime player.'

"So 1946 became an assignment for me. I had to show them. Even before we left for Lakeland, I told my wife: 'I'm not going to be spending much time with you this spring.'

"You have to be a special woman to put up with being married to an athlete, and she's done it for 51 years. But that year had to be the toughest one on her, because everything I had I gave to the game. I had very little left over.

"Every game became a test for me, the chance to show that I belonged. Looking back on it, that year probably shortened my career. I never threw quite as hard after that, I never was quite as intense. But 1946 — that was the year."

At the end, he had won one more game than in the MVP year of 1945, with a 26-9 record, leading the league. His 1.94 earned run average was also the best.

And the only reason his 275 strikeouts didn't lead, too, was because Feller went bonkers and set what was then the strikeout record in the live-ball era with 348.

"Maybe it was that season that I was sitting in the dugout with Stubby Overmire and he mentioned that with a few more years like that I could make the Hall of Fame," he says. "That's the first time it ever entered my mind."

✦ ✦ ✦

95

Mickey *Lolich*

MICKEY LOLICH ✦ LEFT-HAND PITCHER ✦ 1963-1975

Workhorse Lolich could always be counted on to finish what he started

By Jerry Green ✦ *The Detroit News*
ORIGINALLY PRINTED MARCH 31, 1997

Mickey Lolich jumped high and alighted in the hug of Bill Freehan and his catcher's armor at the end of an improbable World Series. The Tigers then swirled onto the St. Louis diamond in the traditional pummeling, pounding, rolling celebration of a world championship.

It had been an improbable World Series, indeed. The Tigers had been down to the Cardinals, with three losses in the first four games and were behind in the fifth game. From that deficit, they won the fifth game, then the sixth and the seventh. In Game 7, the Tigers beat Bob Gibson, who was going for his third victory of the World Series.

Instead, Mickey Lolich ended up with his third victory in the Series.

Like yesterday? Not quite.

"You remember it?" Lolich asked his caller, his biting humor engaged as ever.

"It was 30 years ago."

Do you?

"Do I?" said Lolich. "It hasn't happened since."

And that is a statistical fact. Baseball has not been treat-

Mickey Lolich is third in victories and strikeouts among Tigers pitchers.

ed to a pitcher winning three games In a World Series in the 30 seasons since the Tigers won their 1968 championship.

There are other impressive facts. In that World Series, Lolich finished what he started in all three victories. He pitched nine innings, without relief.

He pitched three complete games — in a period of nine days.

Complete games, the vanishing stat, once upon a time were considered a standard of pitching excellence.

In one season, 1971, Lolich had 29 complete games in a 25-14 season. The next season he pitched 23 complete games with a 22-14 record. In 1974, he had 27 complete games.

In contrast, Pat Hentgen, the Blue Jays' Cy Young Award winner from near Lolich's digs in Macomb County, led major-league baseball in complete-game performances last season. Hentgen finished what he started in 10 games.

Through his 16 sessions, Lolich was a craftsman on the mound. He'd ride to the ballpark on his motorcycle, do his job in two hours or so and hop back onto his bike for the ride home. Today his knowledge of the pitching craft, and his theories, are vivid but defiant against the current trends, while he still rides his bikes.

"I hate to refer to the olden days," Lolich said, "but when I was pitching, the best pitchers on the team were the starting pitchers. The next best were the relievers.

"Nowadays, the closers are the best pitchers. The set-up men who come in to hold the lead until the closers can come in are the next best—and by the way, we need somebody to start the game. Who shall it be?

"But that has come about because of managerial decisions. They've decided it's the way the game is played now.

"If you took a guy like me today, put me in my prime with 40 starts, I'd be gone if I was leading 4-2, out by the sixth inning. If I was behind 4-2, I'd definitely be out."

A key moment in the fifth game of that 1968 World Series occurred in the bottom of seventh inning with the Tigers on the brink of elimination. With one out,

Tom Gage on Mickey Lolich

They don't make pitchers like Mickey Lolich anymore. All those innings, how did he ever do it?

"It's the way we pitched back then," Lolich said. "We had four starters in the rotation, not five. We didn't miss turns."

Some did. But not Lolich. What a workhorse.

Nowadays it's an accomplishment for a starting pitcher to throw 200 innings. They think they've done their job if they reach 200 innings. With bullpens set up the way they are, it's simply the way things are.

But Lolich was just getting started when he reached 200 innings.

Think of it. For four consecutive seasons, he threw more than 300 innings. One year, incredibly enough, he threw 376 innings.

Yet what do we really remember him for? Not for one particular pitch, but for his leap into Bill Freehan's arms.

Bottom of the ninth, seventh game of the 1968 World Series against the St. Louis Cardinals. Mike Shannon had just hit a home run, but who cares, Lolich was still in control.

And there it was, a pop-up off the bat of Tim McCarver, Freehan camping under it for the final out, followed by big Mickey jumping into Freehan's arms as the celebration began.

It was one of the great moments in Tigers' history. Still is, in fact.

and the Tigers a run behind, Lolich was due to bat. Mayo Smith, the manager, defied baseball logic by rejecting the use of a pinch-hitter for his pitcher.

"That's because I was the best pitcher he had at the time," said Lolich.

Lolich, of course, singled to right, starting the rally that won the game and prolonged the Series.

Depressed about modern major-league pitching?

"Yes," said Lolich.

"The split-finger fastball has ruined baseball.

"All pitches, the fastball, curveball and slider, are thrown for strikes. The split-finger is thrown for balls.

Lolich had three complete-game victories in the 1968 World Series.

"Pitchers are always behind with the split-finger. When they're behind, they hit them out of the park."

The result is rising earned-run averages. Today, a 4.00 ERA is a standard for skilled pitching. In the major leagues last season, the aggregate ERA was 4.60.

In Lolich's era, a respectable ERA was 3.00. Lolich had ERA's as low as 2.50 and 2.92 during his career from 1963 to 1979 with the Tigers, Mets and Padres.

In his career, in which he had 217 victories and 191 losses, his lifetime ERA was 3.44.

"Talking ERA, when I pitched, anything under 3.50 would keep you in the starting rotation," Lolich said. "Above 3.50 would put you in the bullpen.

Anything above (4.00) would put you in the minor leagues. "My basic theory of pitching was, if I kept the ball down low, it would take three singles to score one run.

"I didn't believe in walking people. Make them hit the ball. Two of my first three pitches would be strikes."

❖ ❖ ❖

Lolich strikes back during World Series

By Jerry Green ◆ *The Detroit News*
ORIGINALLY PRINTED JULY 19, 1988

Lolich gets a kiss from daughter Kimberly after winning Game 5.

In midsummer of 1968, Mickey Lolich was a would-be hero in a sour mood. The Tigers were charging in the pennant race. Denny McLain was headed toward victory No. 30. Al Kaline was coming back and Mayo Smith had to figure a scheme to get him into the Tigers' lineup for the World Series.

Lolich viewed it all from the wire dungeon where the spare pitchers sit in the bullpen at Tiger Stadium. He was a pitcher in exile, banished from Smith's starting rotation.

"In '68 I wasn't pitching real well, I think I might have been under .500," Lolich recalled. "Mayo was chewing me out, said he was going to send me to the bullpen for a while.

"It was probably the only time in my life that I came back at a manager and I said: 'Well, last year I was the guy who almost won the pennant for us in '67, and if you're going to win this thing in '68, I'll be the guy who'll probably help you get to the '68 World Series.' And he says: 'You got to prove it to me.' And I said: 'I will.'

"And we sort of had a big argument. And he did send me to the bullpen and I won four games out of the bullpen in an eight-day period.

"He must have thought that was good enough and he put me back into the starting rotation."

Lolich danced in the chorus as this show rolled triumphantly into September.

Lolich's simplicity became the foil to the eccentric antics of McLain. Mickey rode to the ballpark on a motorcycle. That became his single peg for publicity.

McLain would go first when the World Series started in St. Louis. Lolich would pitch the second game, following all the hullabaloo. Bob Gibson quickly outdueled McLain in Game 1 to give the Cardinals the edge.

Next day, Lolich faced Nelson Briles. Lolich hit a towering home run, the only one of his career, and beat the Cardinals to square the Series.

By Game 5, on World Series Monday in Detroit, the

◆ ◆ ◆

100

Left-handed pitcher: Mickey Lolich 1963–75

He pitched with a pot belly, saying, "The only thing running and exercising can do for you is make you healthy."

He was one of the strongest pitchers in the game, working more than 300 innings for four straight years and finishing almost everything he started.

He had seasons of 22 and 25 victories but the pinnacle of his career came when he won three games in the 1968 World Series, beating Bob Gibson in the deciding game.

Lolich was a free spirit who laughed a lot around his teammates and rode a motorcycle to the ball park. He learned to throw left-handed when he broke his right arm as a child.

Lolich's profile

The MVP of the Tigers' dramatic 1968 World Series victory over the St. Louis Cardinals, winning three of the four games and outdueling Bob Gibson in Game 7. ... No. 1 in club history in strikeouts, and No. 3 in victories, games and innings. ... A three-time All-Star. ... Threw more than 300 innings four straight years (1971-74). ... Won 25 games in 1971, losing out in Cy Young voting to Vida Blue of the Athletics. ... Has second-most strikeouts by a left-hander, 13th overall.

Tigers were in a jam. The Cardinals had them three victories to one. The Tigers' pride had been shredded.

They were being clobbered. McLain had been beaten twice by Gibson. It was embarrassing.

This was the mood as Lolich warmed up to pitch. If he lost, the World Series would be over, the Tigers finished.

He was in the midst of his warm-up when he had to stop for the singing of The Star-Spangled Banner. The interruption was disconcerting. It broke Lolich's routine. Jose Feliciano was the singer. He sang a long, lilting, heartfelt soul version of the national anthem — rocking and rolling the lyrics — as it never had been done before. The crowd was stunned.

And Lolich was unsettled by the break in his routine. He was behind 3-0 after the first four Cardinals had batted in the first inning. He found a groove then and the Tigers got two back. They were not quite dead.

In the top of the fifth Lolich was in trouble again — and Smith was about to lift him from the game. Lou Brock was on second. Brock raced for the plate on Julian Javier's single to left. Willie Horton fielded the ball in left and gunned it to Bill Freehan at the plate. Freehan blocked Brock off the plate and tagged him out.

The Tigers still trailed 3-2 in the bottom of the seventh. With one out, Lolich was the scheduled batter.

"When I walked from the on-deck circle toward the plate, I looked back over my shoulder and saw that Gates Brown had a bat in his hand," Lolich recalled.

"But Mayo never called me back. The first pitch was a ball and I looked over again. Mayo didn't make a move.

"I got a base hit which started a rally."

The Tigers won Game 5 and returned to St. Louis. Promising not to use McLain again in the Series, Smith changed his mind. In the rain, the Tigers treated McLain to a 10-run rally in the third. The Series was going to be pushed to a seventh game.

After the rally, as Game 6 continued, Smith approached Lolich in the dugout.

"Can you pitch tomorrow?" Smith said.

"Well, Mayo, it's only two days' rest," Lolich said.

"Well, I really want you to start tomorrow," Smith said. "I want you to pitch five innings. Do you think you can pitch five?"

"Yeah, I guess so," said Lolich.

Two decades later, Lolich takes up the story.

"When I came in after five, he asked me could I go one more. Which I did.

"When I came in at the end of the sixth, can you go one more? And then we scored the three runs in the seventh and he asked me if I could finish and I said, 'Yeah.'

"I never thought I was going to pitch in the seventh game."

◆ ◆ ◆

John *Hiller*

John Hiller ✦ Relief Pitcher ✦ 1965-70, 1972-80

Hiller took relief position to new heights after his famed comeback

By Jerry Green ✦ *The Detroit News*
Originally printed May 31 1980

The heart never gave out, but the arm did. "When I was going good," John Hiller said on the night of his mid-season retirement from baseball, "music from the Top Ten was flying through my head. I'd be singing out there on the mound."

This is a beautiful man, a man of courage. You talk about bravery in sports. It is regarded as a display of valor for a shortstop to stand up and cover the bag when a base runner comes in with his spikes high.

Quarterbacks are called gutty when they refuse to duck as two hungry defensive tackles attempt to turn them to mincemeat. Goalies face the slapshot and they are regarded as the bravest of all athletes. And the race car drivers risk death every time they step on the gas.

But all that is toy bravery when compared with John Hiller's feat of courage.

He faced death in real life and laughed about it forever after. In our culture, we look at athletes for inspirational guidance.

A home run in the World Series is worth getting a candy bar to commemorate the hero. The guy who throws the winning pass in the Super Bowl gets a sports car as his personal trophy. But there has never been an athlete who provided more inspiration for the plain people than John Hiller.

He was a fat kid with a buoyant personality and a carefree attitude the day he was struck down. He didn't give much of a damn about anything. Except pitching. That turned him into another guy. It was a tense experience. His nerves twitched when he stood on the mound facing the hitters.

Then he was torn by the searing pain in his chest.

This was the January of 1971. It burned and ached. A heart attack. He was only 27 at the time. Medical science saved his life. The surgeons sliced yards of tubing out of his stomach. Every doctor he talked to told

✦ ✦ ✦

When John Hiller returned to the Tigers 18 months after his heart attack, he made his mark as the best relief pitcher in baseball.

"That's my strongest memory," Hiller said last night at the end of his career. "Richie Allen hitting the home run way up there. My first game after the heart attack. I was just glad to be there."

Hiller became the best relief pitcher in baseball in the years after his return. It was his job to enter the game at the most critical moment. Usually, there were base runners in scoring positions and the score was tight. The game could be won or lost on the next pitch. Hiller would run to the mound and pat his left hand in the pocket of his glove.

"I was always relaxed," Hiller would say, "no matter what the situation was. I never felt tense. It never worried me what I did out there. Why should I? If they beat me, they beat me. I'd gone through something that was a lot worse."

They seldom beat him when he was the top relief pitcher in the game. Hiller loved the routine. He would amble out to the trench where the relief pitchers sat awaiting the next emergency.

John would sit there and swap ribald stories with the others. His were always the best and he was happy when a new pitcher joined the club. It meant a new batch of stories.

About the fourth or fifth inning, Hiller would slip out of the bullpen and tiptoe into the clubhouse. It was time for ice cream on a stick. Jim Campbell finally had the ice cream removed from the clubhouse freezer

him he never could play baseball again. He was lucky to be alive.

Every doctor failed to realize the enormous quantity of courage John Hiller had in his salvaged heart. Eighteen months after the heart attack, Hiller stood on the pitcher's mound at Comiskey Park, Chicago. The fat had been shed with the tubing inside him. But the arm was sound. He was back. He let go a fast ball.

Dick Allen hit it out of the ball park in dead center, 450 feet from the plate. Hiller watched the rocket return to earth and then he turned around and laughed. It was joyous laughter.

Hiller's 2.83 ERA is sixth in team history.

TOM GAGE ON JOHN HILLER

Imagine having a heart attack when you're 27. It happens. Just ask John Hiller.

But instead of feeling sorry for himself, Hiller met the setback with a fierce determination to bounce back and continue his baseball career.

And what a success story it turned out to be. Hiller didn't just continue his career. It was almost as if he began it all over again. But this time as a relief pitcher instead of a starter.

You know the rest. Hiller enjoyed several fine seasons as the Tigers' closer and was the team's all-time leader in saves with 124 until Mike Henneman passed him.

Hiller wasn't just a pitcher, though. He was an inspiration, an example that setbacks can be overcome. I remember watching him one day in 1974 when the Tigers weren't good anymore. Hiller was struggling with his control late in a game against Texas. His fastball wasn't particularly fast this day, nothing much was working for him. The walks began to pile up, so did the scoring chances.

But he did not give in. And the Tigers won the game. Then again, Hiller never gave in. To this day, he has a beautiful perspective on life. He lives way up in the Upper Peninsula, enjoying each day.

Winter can get pretty cold where Hiller lives, but no matter. What's a few flurries to a man who's overcome bigger personal storms than that?

to thwart Hiller's raids.

So John found a new bullpen amusement. He took a portable television out to the pen with him. It helped ease the waiting until the manager needed him to save the game.

"My favorite show was 'The Incredible Hulk,'" Hiller said. "Now it is all over. It happens to all pitchers. The arm goes dead.

"It became a struggle to throw a fastball," said John Hiller, last of the Tigers from the 1968 champions.

"My arm has pitched all it's going to pitch."

His heart never gave out. Only his arm did.

✦ ✦ ✦

Hiller comebacks had serious, light side

By Angelique S. Chengelis ✦ *The Detroit News*
Originally printed August 26, 1986

John Hiller's statistical career

Year	W-L	IP	H	HR	SO	ERA
1965	0-0	6	5	0	4	0.00
1966	0-0	2	2	0	1	9.00
1967	4-3	65	57	4	49	2.63
1968	9-6	128	92	9	78	2.39
1969	4-4	99	97	13	74	3.99
1970	6-6	104	82	12	89	3.03
1972	1-2	44	39	4	26	2.03
1973	10-5	125	89	7	124	1.44
1974	17-14	150	127	10	134	2.64
1975	2-3	70	52	6	87	2.17
1976	12-8	121	93	7	117	2.38
1977	8-14	124	120	15	115	3.56
1978	9-4	92	64	6	74	2.34
1979	4-7	79	83	14	46	5.22
1980	1-0	30	38	3	18	4.40

John Hiller always liked to have fun.

He spent 15 seasons with the Tigers, and the left-hander was usually the one who instigated all the pranks.

One day in Baltimore, Hiller showed up to pitch wearing a wig. To ease the boredom in the bullpen, he'd smuggle in a television. He had a good time being sarcastic and poking fun at the guys, always knowing when enough was enough.

But after six seasons, the converted Canadian was suddenly forced from the game he loved. It came as a shock to the Tigers and their fans, but it was especially shocking to John Hiller.

The date was Jan. 11, 1971, and he began experiencing pain in his arms and chest. Five hours later, the chest pains had subsided, but, he didn't know what was happening to his arms.

The pain was still there. Hiller was having a heart attack, but he didn't know it. He was 27.

Hiller had always been a bit on the heavy side; he was an imposing figure on the mound. But at 6-1, 220 pounds, he wasn't a very healthy athlete.

He spent five weeks in the hospital; his doctors said he'd never play baseball again.

In April of 1971, Hiller had surgery, moving seven feet of his intestines to lower his cholesterol content and dissolve cholesterol deposits in his arteries.

His weight stabilized to about 175 pounds and he was feeling good. Prior to the operation, Hiller, 23-19 after six seasons of pitching mostly relief, was allowed to spend time as a pitching coach with the Lakeland Tigers in the Florida State League.

There, he pitched the equivalent of two games a week and also threw some batting practice.

By November, Hiller was running, swimming, and exercising as often as he could. His doctors did more tests and found the arteries that had been blocked were clear.

But could he play baseball again? The doctors were still uncertain.

"I knew my career couldn't be over, because I couldn't do anything else," said Hiller. "My doctors said I'd never play, but I said forget it, I have to.

"I had so many people telling me I wouldn't get back. But I worked my butt off. I quit smoking and drinking and psychologically, what I went through really helped me."

But it didn't help the Tigers. When Hiller came back in 1972, he wanted to go to spring training as a player, not a pitching coach.

Potential trouble didn't bother Billy Martin, who became manager the year Hiller was out.

By the middle of July, 1972, Martin activated him and began using Hiller in a short relief role. He

✦ ✦ ✦

Relief pitcher:
John Hiller 1965-70, 1972-80

No one ever turned his life around more than the veteran left-hander. He was a free spirit, paying little attention to the rules of life, but straightened out after suffering a heart attack in the middle of his career.

He came back to become the game's premier reliever over the objections of his boss, General Manager Jim Campbell, who did did not want him to pitch again after his heart problems.

Hiller simply didn't listen, and became the heart of the pitching staff at a time when the Tigers were struggling to look respectable. He saved 125 games, second to Mike Henneman's 154 saves.

Hiller's highlights

Appeared in more games than any other pitcher who ever wore a Tiger uniform. ... Named to one all-star game. ... had a then-record 38 saves in 1973, when he compiled a 10-5 record and a 1.44 ERA in 65 appearances, all the more amazing since he suffered a heart attack in 1971. ... Earned AL Comeback Player of the Year and Fireman of the Year honors in 1973.

Hiller retired in 1980 at age 37.

appeared in 24 games, pitched 44 innings and completed one game in three starts.

But during that time, Hiller also found that his fastball was much better and the change-up he'd worked on the spring before was becoming his most effective pitch. By 1973 he was able to use them quite frequently, and he had earned a spot on the roster as a reliever.

"I liked the idea of relief pitching," Hiller said. He was very good in that role that year, pitching 125 innings in 65 games with 124 strikeouts.

Yet the most impressive statistic was Hiller's 38 saves — an American League record that stood until Kansas City's Dan Quisenberry had 45 saves in 1983.

Hiller was named Tiger of the Year and Comeback Player of the Year, and finished fourth in the A.L. Cy Young award voting, the only reliever to receive votes. And those were just a few of the awards heaped on him after that remarkable season.

In his seven remaining years in baseball, Hiller never had a season like that one, but in 1974 he had a 17-14 record in relief and saved 13 games. He also was one of two relievers selected to the All-Star game.

✦ ✦ ✦

Shoulda' Been Contenders

Player-manager Mickey Cochrane led the
Tigers to their first World Series title in 1935.

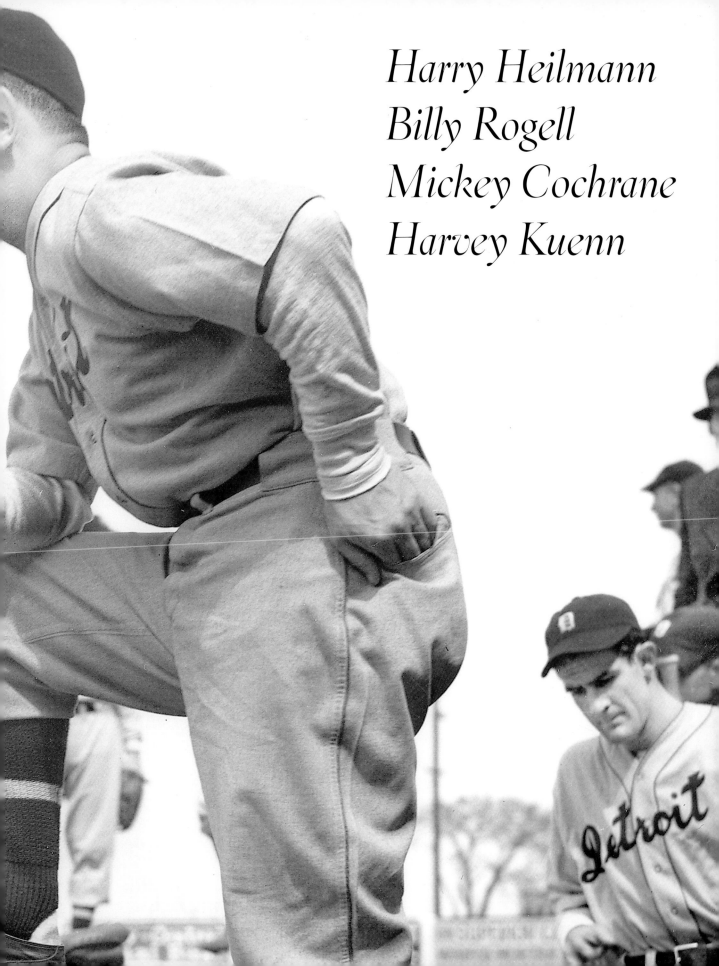

Harry Heilmann
Billy Rogell
Mickey Cochrane
Harvey Kuenn

Heilmann deserves a spot on team

By Joe Falls ✦ *The Detroit News*
ORIGINALLY PRINTED SEPTEMBER 27, 1999

Who is Harry Heilmann? Good question. Our fans today not only have forgotten him, but many also have never heard of him. "Harry who?" was the most common reaction among the fans who attended Sunday's game at Tiger Stadium. Too bad.

What Tigers fans did was remove Heilmann from the all-time Tigers team and replace him with Kirk Gibson.

Come on, folks. No one expects you to remember what happened 70 or so years ago, but history is history and should never be forgotten.

That would be like saying Abraham Lincoln doesn't count anymore because he was president 135 years ago.

So, let's put it as simply as possible.

Heilmann, who played from 1914-32, in the Ty Cobb era, had a career batting average of .342, 10th-best on the major-league list.

From 1919-1929 with the Tigers, Heilmann batted .320, .309, .394, .356, .403, .346, .393, .367, .398, .328 and .344, and won batting titles in 1921, '23, '25 and '27.

Gibson had a career average of .278 and never came close to a batting title.

This is not meant as a knock on Gibson, who was a winner when he played. It is an example of how the fans of today relate to what they see, not what they are told. If it doesn't appear on SportsCenter, it hasn't happened.

"I understand it," Gibson said. "I have two feelings about making the team. I could not be more pleased than to stand next to Al Kaline and George Kell. But I also know why it happened. The fans who voted for me did not do any research. I appreciate their support but I also know what happened. Even I don't know anything about Harry Heilmann.

"The only thing that matters in baseball is whether you win or lose. I've always thought of myself as an average player who was a winner. I had an impact on the game. I took a lot of heat — some of it my fault — but I always stood up to be counted, both for myself and my teammates.

"If I had to act a little extreme at times to take the pressure off them, I did it. I considered myself a complete team player."

Heilmann spent 34 years with the Tigers — 17 as a player and 17 as a broadcaster. Most of those who recognized his name remembered him from his radio broadcasts. Most never heard of him.

Said Brian McGwire, a 46-year-old Tigers fan: "I don't know who he is."

Said Tony Dragos, 72: "All I remember is hearing him on the radio."

Said Pat Sponkle, 37: "I never heard of him."

It was left to Karen Bush, 58, to put it all into perspective: "All this is is a cheap way to market the modern game."

The Tigers say more than 25,000 fans voted, but did not announce the totals, only percentages.

✦ ✦ ✦

Harry Heilmann was a master with a bat, hitting over .390 on four occasions and winning four batting titles.

The voting doesn't make a lot of sense. For instance, when the all-time Tigers team was picked for the first time in 1969, Billy Rogell was the shortstop. Now, Harvey Kuenn has moved ahead of Rogell and into second behind Alan Trammell, though Kuenn and Rogell haven't done a thing in the past 30 years.

A 79-year-old man in Dearborn was asked about Heilmann's rebuff. He said: "I understand it, but he'll always be on my team."

The speaker was, Harry Heilmann Jr.

◆ ◆ ◆

Heilmann was a magician at bat

By H.G. Salsinger ✦ *The Detroit News*
ORIGINALLY PRINTED JULY 10, 1951

When they carried Harry Heilmann into Morrell Memorial Hospital in Lakeland on a stretcher last March, after he collapsed in his hotel room, he said: "This is it."

A few days later he was told: "The X-ray films show some very bad spots on your lungs and they may indicate any one of four ailments, all very serious, but a complete diagnosis will be necessary to determine which one." A few weeks later he was brought to Detroit by plane and entered Henry Ford Hospital. After the doctors finished their test he called us up.

"Remember when the doctors in Lakeland told me — about the spots on my lungs indicating one of four serious ailments? Well, I've just found out that it's the worst of the four. I'm through and I wanted you to be the first to know it." "After announcing that he was mortally ill, he told a funny story concerning a mutual friend and laughed.

A fitting headline for news of his death would be: "A Game Guy Passes."

Courage he had, rare courage, the kind that few men have. He knew that death would come any day, any hour, and he mentioned it frequently, but his spirit never faltered.

He would recall some baseball incident and relate it in a voice that constantly grew weaker, and laugh. He told us: People have been so nice to me, so generous and gra-

HARRY EDWIN HEILMANN
DETROIT, A.L.-CINCINNATI, N.L.
1916-1932
RIGHT HANDED HITTING OUTFIELDER AND
FIRST BASEMAN, WON AMERICAN LEAGUE
BATTING CHAMPIONSHIP FOUR TIMES
1921, '23, '25 AND '27. IN 1923, BATTED .403.
COLLECTED 2660 HITS AND 183 HOME RUNS
IN 2,146 MAJOR LEAGUE GAMES. HAD
LIFETIME BATTING AVERAGE OF .342 AND
FIELDING MARK OF .975.

cious that I feel ashamed, for I don't deserve all the grand things done in my behalf.

He was a humble man and a great one. Ty Cobb called him one of the best two righthanded hitters in the history of baseball.

When his playing days ended, he became one of the best three baseball broadcasters in the country. He never regarded himself as a great ballplayer nor a good broadcaster, but he was both.

His own popularity puzzled him, but it puzzled none who knew him intimately. He had most of the human virtues. He was kind, generous, honest, sincere, loyal, forgiving, tolerant and understanding.

He has a lifetime batting average of .342, the same as Babe Ruth, who was his close friend during the years that both were trying to lead the league in hitting.

Heilmann won four batting championships and his pal, Babe, won one. Only Cobb won more American league batting titles than Heilmann. Heilmann topped the league with .394 in 1921, .403 in 1923, .393 in 1925 and .398 in 1927.

In those four seasons, he made 874 hits in 2,204 times at bat for a remarkable average of .397. In the last

✦ ✦ ✦

20 years only Ted Williams (in 1941) equaled or surpassed Hailmann's lowest title-winning average of .393.

Heilmann had complete confidence in himself. Moe Berg, who was catching for the Chicago White Sox in the '20s, said: "There were times when it seemed that Heilmann could lead the American League any time he wanted to, or pick out the year in which he wanted to hit .400. He couldn't, of course, but that was the impression he gave you when he was in one of those batting streaks of his."

He also credited Ty Cobb with developing him as a hitter. It was Cobb who taught him to hit with his feet close together and to grip his bat far down at the end.

Standing at the plate, with the bat resting against the hollow of his right shoulder, Heilmann was a menacing figure who seemed to look right through the pitcher and dare him to throw the ball within striking distance.

During one of his batting streaks, he hit three home runs in two games in Boston. We asked him why he did not go in for home runs.

"Home runs are Babe Ruth's specialty. He gets paid for hitting them, and people come to the ball parks to see him hit them. Even if I hit 75 home runs in one year, it wouldn't help me much. There would still be the base, and people would resent my intrusion."

No longer will radio listeners hear the familiar, "This is your Goebel baseball reporter, Harry Heilmann speaking." The voice to which millions lis-

Harry Heilmann won four batting championships while rival Babe Ruth won only one.

tened to eagerly in the last 10 years has been stilled forever. He had a personal charm and his broadcasts did more to attract people to Briggs Stadium than the Detroit club ever realized or appreciated.

❖ ❖ ❖

Rogell gets it going with defense

By H.G. Salsinger ✦ *The Detroit News*
ORIGINALLY PRINTED SEPTEMBER 11, 1935

There are days when he looks like a minor leaguer. Bill Rogell has the mechanical equipment to make him the best man at his position in decades, but he lacks the necessary temperament.

He is the victim of moods and at times he sulks and wishes that he had never taken up baseball as a profession.

On those days he would much rather be somewhere else.

But on the days when the mood is upon him and he feels the lure of the game Rogell gives dazzling performances.

He is sure and he is spectacular.

No batter can hit a ball through him; no batter can hit a ball anywhere near him and get it by.

Not as good a thrower as Joe Cronin (who is the best throwing infielder in the league), Rogell is still one of the best. He covers more territory than any of them and he has no equal in fielding a badly hopping ball.

Originally an outfielder for Coffeyville, where he started his professional career in 1923, Rogell can travel probably farther for fly balls than any contemporary and is a safer bet in catching them. He is a firm protector of the short left field territory.

He is a firm believer in hunches. Nearly all of his brilliant performances have been given in games where he hit safely on his first time at bat. Let Rogell get a hit the first time up and he becomes convinced that the day is his and that everything will break for him. Everything generally does break for him, but only because Rogell creates the breaks. He moves over the short field territory on those days with supreme confidence, tries for everything, breaks with the ball and will take care of any chance that could be handled by any shortstop of any period.

His lapses come on the days when he fails on his first time up, or on his first or second time at bat; when he is called out on a bad strike, or pops a foul fly, or hits a ball perfectly only to have some fielder haul it in.

These are the breaks that toss Rogell into deep gloom and when they continue for two or three games he becomes morose and thinks that luck has turned definitely against him. His fielding becomes bad. He starts late after batted balls, he plays wrong position, he makes mechanical and tactical errors.

If Rogell could ignore the bad breaks at bat and concentrate on the fielding, he would be one of the outstanding stars of the game, but his brilliant performances are always paralleled by his careless exhibitions.

There is no consistency to his play; if there were he would stand alone among the best shortstops of his league.

Yet I have never seen a shortstop go further to his left than Rogell does. He has no equal in picking up a ball while on a dead run and throwing while off balance.

He is excellent on a double play, either in starting it or acting as pivot. He is good going to his right and will also go deep to his right, and nail many well-hit balls.

The Tigers purchased Rogell from St. Paul in 1930, but

✦ ✦ ✦

Billy Rogell finally made a believer of Tigers manager Bucky Harris with his performance.

he didn't last long. When he reported to camp in the spring he was ambushed by utility infielder Bill Akers.

One day, while the Detroit infield was working out at Navin Field, prior to a game, Akers strolled to the shortstop position where Rogell was fielding grounders.

Akers told Rogell: "I'm playing shortstop and you can take a rest. (manager Bucky) Harris told me I was to be the shortstop from now on."

When Harris arrived in the dugout he found Rogell sitting gloomily in a corner. Out on the field was Akers practicing on the shortstop position.

"Why aren't you out there?" Harris asked Rogell.

"Akers told me he was playing shortstop from now on," explained Rogell.

Harris decided that if Rogell let a substitute like Akers chase him from his job it would probably be wise to let Akers continue at the position. Any player with that amount of nerve should succeed.

Rogell was shipped to Toronto and Akers continued at shortstop, but not for long. Harris soon found out that nerve was Akers' only asset as a major leaguer.

In 1931 Detroit was still looking for a shortstop. The scouting reports said that the best shortstop in the minors was playing at Toronto. His name was Rogell.

Harris, still influenced by the Akers incident, did not want Rogell.

"There surely must be a better one somewhere. It isn't possible that he's the best in the minor leagues," Harris commented.

But there was not a better one in the minor leagues, and Detroit finally bought back Rogell, paying $10,000 cash for a player who had been virtually given to Toronto as a present the previous year.

Rogell played 48 games for Detroit in 1931, and at the close of the season Harris remarked:

"I was wrong. Rogell is really a shortstop and he can become the best in baseball. Some transformation must have taken place while he was in Toronto."

And if Rogell gets complete confidence and can forget the bad breaks at bat and change his temperament to the extent where that is possible, he will be without a peer. He has everything in a mechanical way that his contemporaries lack.

◆ ◆ ◆

Cochrane owned Detroit in 1935

By H.G. Salsinger ✦ *The Detroit News*
ORIGINALLY PRINTED AUG. 7, 1938

For two seasons Mickey Cochrane was the idol of the Detroit public. When he came here from Philadelphia in 1934, he supplied the Tigers with magnetic leadership. What probably was more important, he gave them an aggressive catcher for the first time in a dozen or more years.

The combination lifted Detroit to its first American League pennant since 1909. Defeat by the St. Louis Cardinals in the World Series followed, but the next season, Cochrane drove the Tigers to both the pennant and world championship.

He scored the run, on Goose Goslin's single, that gave Detroit the deciding game over the Chicago Cubs in the post-season series.

With a championship under his belt, Cochrane was the toast of the town. It looked as if he would lead the Tigers indefinitely. A grateful citizenship acclaimed his genius, called him "miracle man" and turned confidently to 1936 with the hope that the Tigers would become one of the few teams in history to win three successive pennants.

But ill luck of several kinds overtook Cochrane. Several of his key players, including Hank Greenberg, were injured. Schoolboy Rowe developed trouble with his arm.

Cochrane himself was taken seriously ill and had to leave the club for a vacation and rest in Wyoming. He resumed command before the season ended and the

GORDON "MICKEY" COCHRANE
PHILADELPHIA A.L. 1925-1933
DETROIT A.L. 1934-1937
FIERY CATCHER COMPILED A NOTABLE
RECORD BOTH AS A PLAYER AND MANAGER.
THE SPARK OF THE ATHLETICS' CHAMPIONSHIP
TEAMS OF 1929-30-31, HAD AN AVERAGE
BATTING MARK OF .346 FOR THOSE THREE
YEARS. LED DETROIT TO TWO LEAGUE
CHAMPIONSHIPS AND A WORLD SERIES
TITLE IN 1935.

Tigers finished second to the Yankees.

In 1937 Cochrane attempted a comeback as a catcher. He was successful until felled by a pitched ball by Bump Hadley in Yankee Stadium on May 25.

For weeks, he lay between life and death in a New York hospital. He finally recovered and returned to the dugout as manager but his health kept him out of the lineup.

After he was forced to the sidelines, Cochrane apparently lost some of his skill as a leader. As a bench manager he could not rally the Tigers for a consistent drive as he had been able to do when in the thick of the fight himself.

Without Cochrane setting a personal pace, the club lagged and fell far behind the leaders.

Cochrane's job with Detroit was his first as manager. He came here from Philadelphia after establishing himself as the greatest catcher of the modern period; if not of all time. He strengthened his rank while catching for the Tigers. Detroit never had a catcher to compare with him.

As a handler of pitchers, it is doubtful that

✦ ✦ ✦

Two champions — Cochrane and Joe Louis — ham it up at a Tigers game.

judge a pitched ball. Charlie Gehringer is probably the only other player in the game today who was the equal or superior of Cochrane in hitting a ball after two strikes have been called.

To Cochrane, like Gehringer, two strikes meant nothing; to other players it generally means a slight change in grip or stance, or both, and tightening to a certain extent. Two strikes never handicapped Cochrane, never caused him to offer at a bad pitch to keep from striking out. Pitchers had to make the "big one" good for Cochrane.

No other catcher in the game has had the same success in working pitchers. Tommy Bridges had a great deal of stuff but never won 20 games a season before Cochrane came to Detroit. He won 46 during the first three years of Cochrane's managerial career.

Cochrane caught Schoolboy Rowe into a string of 16 consecutive victories, tying the modern pitching championship. He took on Alvin Crowder, after he was labeled as through in 1934, and made Crowder a most important factor in two successful pennant fights.

Mechanically he had no equal. While most old-time catchers walk around with gnarled fingers, Cochrane never had a finger injury.

He changed the style of receiving, letting the glove do the catching and the hand do the holding. He caught so that the ball always landed in the socket of the mitt and let his bare hand close over it. No catcher had this trick before Cochrane came along.

He probably never had an equal tagging runners coming into the plate.

Cochrane ever had a superior in the major leagues. He worked along the simple lines he had learned from the master, Connie Mack.

It was under Cochrane's handling that Schoolboy Rowe, Tommy Bridges and Elden Auker had their best seasons. Cochrane had a way with pitchers rarely equaled.

Cochrane was voted the most valuable player in the American League in 1928, when he was with Philadelphia and again in 1934, when he was with Detroit. He was the most valuable catcher in nearly all of his active seasons.

Cochrane and Roger Bresnahan were the only two catchers in baseball history who were fast enough to be placed first in the batting order.

Cochrane had everything that the ideal catcher should have — and speed to boot. In addition to his uncommon speed Cochrane had the unusual ability to

Kuenn's best days were with Tigers

By Mike O'Hara ✦ *The Detroit News*
ORIGINALLY PRINTED JUNE 24, 1986

S oon, they would be lining up at a table that had been placed on a small, elevated platform in a corner of a ballroom at the Roma Hall in West Bloomfield. The prize was Harvey Kuenn's autograph — one signature on a scrap of paper, baseball or picture, at four bucks a throw.

The setting was a sports memorabilia show for people who like to swap baseball cards for a price and buy such other baseball artifacts as Al Kaline's road jersey, a reproduction of Kuenn and Kaline on the cover of *Sports Illustrated* in 1956, and Lou Brock's baseball bat. For a cool $1,000, you can have Kaline's jersey. Kuenn's 1959 baseball card goes for $4. And for $10, a 1983 Los Angeles Dodgers puzzle is all yours.

Zounds.

But the real gem at the Roma was Kuenn's honest-to-gosh signature. As the line grew in the ballroom, Kuenn talked baseball — some of it about himself, about life in Detroit, and about a day in the spring of 1960 that he will never forget.

When he thinks of 1960, Kuenn thinks of The Trade.

Kuenn had played five innings of the Tigers' last exhibition game in Florida that spring. It was April 17. The next day the Tigers were to fly to Cleveland, where they would open the season against the Indians on April 19.

After one of the biggest trades in the Tigers' history, Kuenn played on Opening Day — for the Cleveland Indians. Gone was the man who had led the American League in hitting in 1959, with a .353 average. In his place, the Tigers had Rocky Colavito, a home run hitter and community idol in Cleveland.

"It was the most shocking thing that ever happened to me in baseball," Kuenn said. "In those days, trades were made like that. You never had anything to say about it. You were just happy to be going to another major-league club."

If Kuenn had had an agent at the time, he never would have gone to Cleveland.

"I'd probably have had it in my contract that I wouldn't be traded," Kuenn said.

He recalled the day's events that severed his connection with the Tigers.

"I'd played five innings of our last exhibition game in Cleveland," he said. "Jimmie Dykes was our manager then. He told me, 'I'd like to see you in my office.' I didn't have any idea what was going on at that point. We just walked back together. There wasn't much said.

"He told me to sit down. He offered me a cigar."

It wasn't quite like finding a dead fish on the front seat of his truck; but Kuenn knew something was afoot. He didn't need a kiss on the cheek. He was traded.

"He wished me well, and I wished Jimmie Dykes well," Kuenn said. "I hated to leave Detroit because I thought we had a chance to win it all.

"I took the cigar."

✦ ✦ ✦

Kuenn left behind a trail of outstanding hitting years in Detroit. He broke in as a full-time shortstop with the Tigers in 1953. He hit .308 with 209 hits. He had 201 hits the next year and hit .306. Only once as a Tiger did Kuenn's average fall below .300 — in 1957, when he hit .277.

Kuenn was never as productive at the plate after he left Detroit. He hit .308 in 1960, his only season with the Indians. Colavito was so popular in Cleveland that there was a backlash against Kuenn. The Indians traded him to San Francisco in 1961 and Kuenn finished out his career in the National League.

Kuenn was a streak hitter in Detroit. Except the streak began on Opening Day and never ended.

At 55, Kuenn's eyes still have the sharp blaze that gave him his ability at the bat.

Time was not altogether kind to Kuenn. He lost part of his right leg because of diabetes, and he underwent open heart surgery.

His last full-time job in baseball was as manager of the Milwaukee Brewers. Kuenn took over for Buck Rodgers during the 1982 season and led Milwaukee to the Brewers' only World Series appearance.

Kuenn was rehired for the 1983 season, but was fired after Milwaukee slumped to fifth place and finished 11 games out of first place.

Kuenn still works as a scout for the Brewers. He scouts the National League teams and helps out in the Instructional League.

It isn't the same pace or grind he endured as a player and manager, but it keeps Kuenn close enough to the game.

"It's a lot of fun," Kuenn said. "But I always said that when it stops being fun, that's when you're in trouble."

Kuenn is as surprised as most other experts that Detroit is in last place in the American League East. He expected Detroit and Toronto to challenge for the division title. He went through the same thing in Milwaukee in 1983 that has happened to Detroit the last two seasons. A good, young team disintegrated rapidly.

Kuenn's batting average fell below .300 once as a Tiger.

"Other ballclubs start to improve a little bit more," Kuenn said. "They get higher draft choices because they weren't winning. Young people come up (on other teams) when you've more or less stuck with the same ballclub."

♦ ♦ ♦

Colorful Characters

Mark Fidrych
Denny McLain
Hughie Jennings

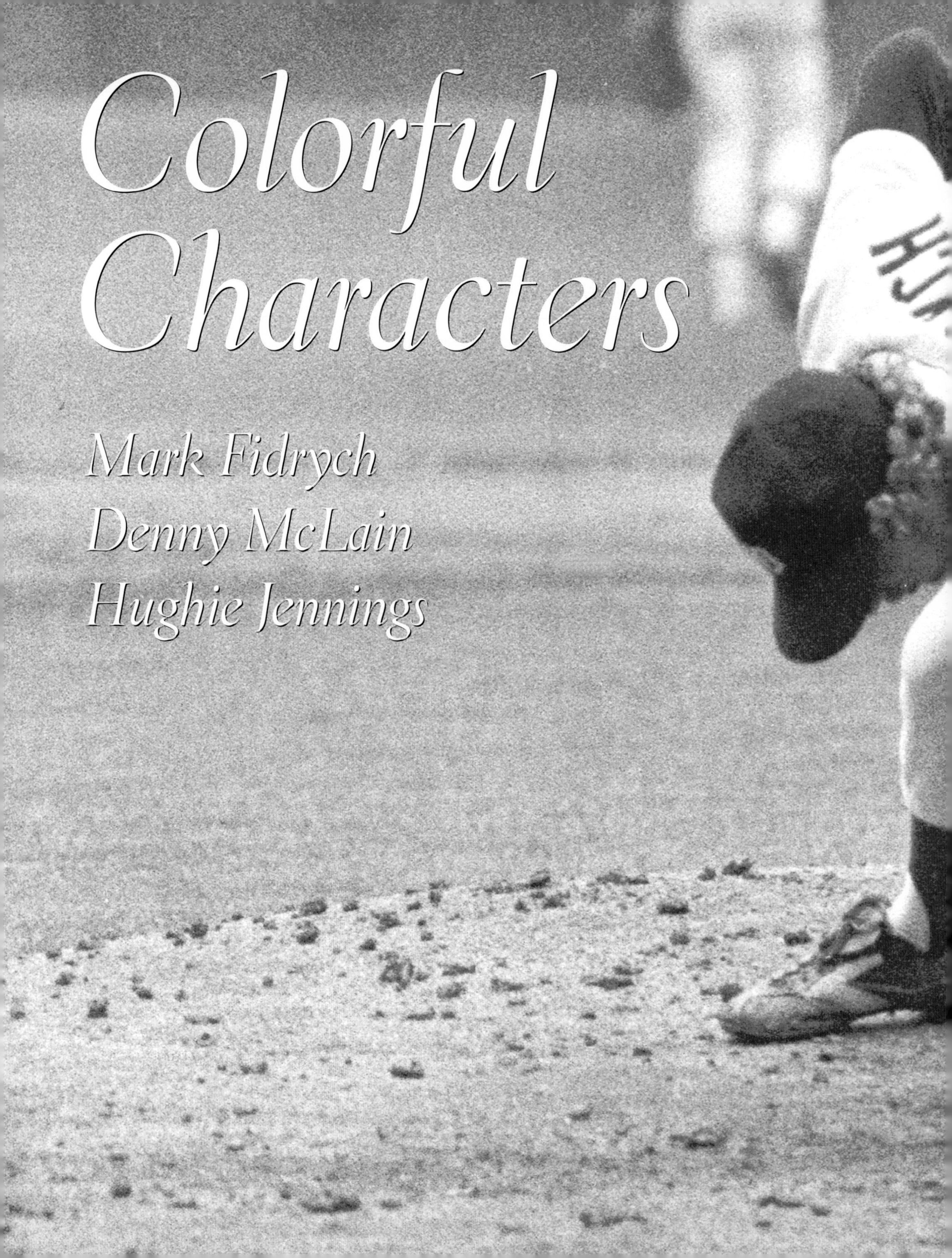

Mark Fidrych did a little groundskeeping in
addition to winning rookie honors in 1976.

Bird's one season was a great one

By Jerry Green ✦ *The Detroit News*
ORIGINALLY PRINTED MARCH 20, 1996

The kid with the screechy voice went to the pay phone in the corner of the spring-training clubhouse. "Got a dime?" he asked the clubhouse boy. It was the same tone he used in his one-sided dialogue with baseballs.

The attendant handed him a coin to raise an operator for the collect call to Massachusetts.

"Mom, dad, I made it," said Mark Fidrych, age 21.

He had a bird's face and long curly yellowish hair and an odd gait and a way about him.

"It's not every day a kid makes it," he said after he completed his call home. "I'm one in a million. I'll tell you, man, it's the rush of my life. I'll never have another high like it. I went to stand up and my legs shook so much I couldn't stand.

"You married? Like when you got married. That's a rush."

It was 20 years ago. Wow — his favorite expression. Just about this time in spring training, the Tigers were in a rebuilding mode, and Ralph Houk, the manager, had decided to take an untested rookie north from Lakeland with them on their pitching staff for the 1976 season.

It was the start of something...

Where is he now, Mark Fidrych, "The Bird," who enchanted American before fading from baseball two broken seasons later with a bum arm and an aching knee?

"He's here," said Jessica Fidrych, age 8, into another telephone in Northborough, Mass. She called her daddy to the phone.

"I still have a 10-wheeler," said Mark Fidrych, age 41,

his voice the same as it had been since the day it had started to change. "A dump truck. I haul asphalt and gravel.

"I was out visiting my friend Larry King in Michigan last weekend. Chesterfield Township. He has a screening plant. A rig that separates rock out of dirt. He's got a gravel train. I'd like to have one for my farm.

"I still have my farm. I do a little work."

Fidrych had just cooked supper — his word — for Jessica and his wife Ann, who works as a nutritionist.

"My life's changed a lot," he said, "and I think it's changed for the better.

"Now you see athletes doing commercials. I'd like to think I'm still marketable. I think there's still a market for me in Detroit.

"I was national at one time. I was like Larry Bird. A Michael Jordan. A Rodman...

"Like Neil Simon said to me once in New York, 'You're an untapped oil well.'"

Fidrych had taken Detroit by storm in the summer of the nation's Bicentennial, winning 19 games and starting in the All-Star Game as a rookie.

Once, Fidrych had a cameo role in playwright/screenwriter Simon's "Slugger's Wife."

One year after his stratospheric season, Fidrych's arm went bad. He hurt the knee climbing the wire fence at Marchant Stadium in Lakeland. He would win

✦ ✦ ✦

only eight more games in 1977 and 1978, appear in only 13 more. His career was done by the time he was 25.

One day he told Fred Gladding, the pitching coach, that he couldn't throw. Tiger Stadium was packed to see him. Another pitcher, a rookie named Jack Morris, went to the bullpen to warm up for his first major-league start. The fans booed Morris. Jim Campbell, the club president, grabbed the public address microphone and explained to the customers that Fidrych could not pitch, that they could have their ticket money back.

"It was a way of showing the fans we're not savages," Fidrych said from Northborough. "I said, 'Jack have fun today, because the fun is over.'"

It was, but it wasn't.

He returned to Northborough, leaving us with baseball stories that belonged to rich fiction.

"Oh, I don't do that anymore," he said this past week. "The Fried Egg."

It was a dance Fidrych and a friend invented once in Northborough and told us about, part of his persona.

"We'd get on our backs and wiggle on the floor," he said. "At Sir Morgan's Cove in Worcester."

The Bird's heart remains in Detroit. He comes here often, for charity events, to participate with Wertz's Warriors in their annual snowmobiling fund-raiser. And as he has done since 1977, he still purchases four season tickets for the ball games at Tiger Stadium, passing them out to friends.

"I'll probably never give them up until I die," he said.

Mark Fidrych took America by storm in 1976, winning 19 games and playing to packed stadiums.

✦ ✦ ✦

McLain was ace of '68 Series team

By Jerry Green ✦ *The Detroit News*
Originally printed 1993

I t was 25 years ago, but the mystique of Denny McLain and the 1968 Tigers still grips those who lived through it all. The swagger and the carefree spirit are still there 25 years later, cemented in the persona of Dennis Dale McLain.

Denny McLain was in a zone in 1968 when he became the last man to win 30 games in a season.

✦ ✦ ✦

124

They remain a quarter-century after his pitching exploits provided an escape for a war-angry nation and an antidote to a riot-frightened city.

"I felt absolutely invincible that year," says McLain, whose stream-of-consciousness gabbiness has rescued him from the ruins of his post-Tigers life.

"The first two games I didn't even get a decision. I knew I was pitching well. Good was an understatement, and the game was so easy.

"If I wanted to throw the ball down-and-away into a spot 2-by-2, it looked 6-by-6. It was that

wide to me. It was doubly easy. No matter how many men got on they weren't going to score. There'd be a strikeout, a line drive, a pop up. They weren't going to score."

This was vintage Denny McLain. The true Denny McLain. Not the voice who has become a popular morning talk-show radio host with a multitude of controversial opinions on WXYT-AM. Not the TV goofball who teams in sports comedy gigs on Channel 2 with Eli Zaret. Not the Denny who strayed and spent time in the federal slammer.

This was Denny as he sounded in 1968, that tragic-wonderful year when the Tigers won a pennant. This was the Denny who ripped the fans for presumed disloyalties, then apologized; the Denny who took off for Las Vegas at the controls of a Learjet; the Denny who played the organ in concert, with groups, once from the loft at Tiger Stadium.

You have to be at least 30 now to remember what the summer was like, that summer of Vietnam War protest and the gunning down of American leaders. Dr. Martin Luther King, killed. Bobby Kennedy, killed.

That summer when Dennis Dale McLain, with his pitching artistry, won 31 games for the Tigers in a town that had burned one year earlier in riots.

"It was such a blur," McLain says 25 years later, now age 49. "It happened so quickly. A couple of good things I remember. The way they celebrated in Detroit. Black, white, green, yellow, they were hugging each other. Next time, they burned the town down. That was '84.

"And fundamentally, it's the best baseball team I've ever seen. You expected us to win every night."

It is vivid still in the imaginations of those of us who were around the ballpark in '68. The '68 Tigers are etched in this community as no other Detroit team, in any sport, can be.

◆ ◆ ◆

Jennings was best before Sparky

By Joe Falls ✦ *The Detroit News*
ORIGINALLY PRINTED SEPTEMBER 2, 1992

He was every bit as colorful as Sparky Anderson — a popular man with the public. Everyone liked Hughie Jennings in his days as manager of the Tigers.

They called him the "Ee-Yah!" man, the man who managed the club for 14 seasons and won three straight pennants in '07, '08 and '09. He was a happy man, a blue-eyed, freckle-faced Irishman who had a fine sense of humor and always seemed to have a grin.

He certainly enriched the lexicon of baseball. Jennings would stand in the first-base coaching box, raise his fists, kick one leg in the air and yell: "Here we are!" Finally, by sacrificing consonants for simplicity, this became "Ee-Yah!" The fans would pick up the chant whenever Jennings would step onto the field, and sounds would ring through old Bennett Park.

Jennings had been a shortstop for the old Baltimore Orioles in the late 1800s and his greatest claim to fame — the one that caught the attention of everyone in baseball — is how well he got along with Ty Cobb. It wasn't easy, because not many ever got along with Cobb. But they survived together for 14 years, before Cobb himself took over from Jennings as manager in 1921.

An educated man who passed his bar examination while managing the Tigers, Jennings was one of the early dugout psychologists who probed the players' psyches to bring out their best. Connie Mack called him one of the three greatest managers in history, along with John McGraw and Joe McCarthy.

As a student at Cornell, where he coached the base-ball team in exchange for his tuition, young Jennings decided to go swimming one evening. It was near dusk, and he didn't bother to turn on the lights in the natatorium. He dived off the high springboard and landed head first on the concrete floor. Again, he survived.

Jennings' special treatment of Cobb didn't sit well with some of the other Tigers. In fact, many resented it.

Jennings was not as easy on some of his other players. He was running a rollicking team but demanded some discipline. One day he ordered first baseman Claude Rossman to lay down a bunt. Rossman crossed up his manager and hit a home run. Jennings fined him $50.

Jennings' psychology may seem rudimentary by today's standards, but it was almost revolutionary at the time. The usual procedure was to threaten a player to make him produce. Jennings' theory was quite the opposite. He said: "Never waste your time and energy scolding a man in anger. When you are angry, your reasoning is not sound. If you must scold, let the man know that by taking up time with him you are paying him the highest compliment possible. If you have to start fining them, it is time to get rid of them."

Cobb was his greatest test.

From the beginning, Cobb was hard to handle — a man who could be insufferable in the way he treated others. He thought of little more than himself. He insisted on

✦ ✦ ✦

126

doing everything his own way.

But almost immediately, Jennings saw brilliance. More important, he recognized young Cobb's individuality. He called Cobb aside one day and said: "There isn't anything about baseball I can teach you. Anything I might say to you would merely hinder you in your development. The only thing for you to do is go ahead and do as you please. Use your own judgment. You can teach yourself better than any man I know can teach you. You just go ahead and work things out your way. Do what you think is best and I'll back you up."

That was all Cobb needed to hear. It set him apart from his teammates, and that was exactly what he wanted. He knew Jennings was a tough player in his day. When he played for the bustling Orioles, Jennings was their most aggressive player. His speciality was getting hit by pitched balls to set up rallies. It was permissible to step in front of pitches in those days, and he would get hit as much as three times in one game. One time, in Philadelphia, he got hit in the head in the third inning, but he finished the game. The moment it was over, he collapsed, unconscious.

Manager Hughie Jennings was a showman, getting the crowd involved with his 'Ee-Yah!' chant.

Jennings would work his psychology on other players, as well. His favorite target was Ed Walsh, the great pitcher of the White Sox. Both came from the same coal-mining neighborhood of Moosic, Pa. Walsh's family was Polish; Jennings' Irish.

Whenever the teams met, Jennings would cry out: "You're not kidding me. You're real name is Wallonski. You stole a good Irish name just as you stole pennies from the poor box in church." Walsh would become unnerved and lose his composure. In Jennings' first year, Walsh won 24 games but couldn't finish any against the Tigers.

After 14 years, Jennings not only was losing interest in the team, but also his nerves. With the team floundering in seventh place in 1920, he could take no more. He knew he could not meet his own standards and told Cobb: "I can't take it any longer. I want you to take over the club."

◆ ◆ ◆

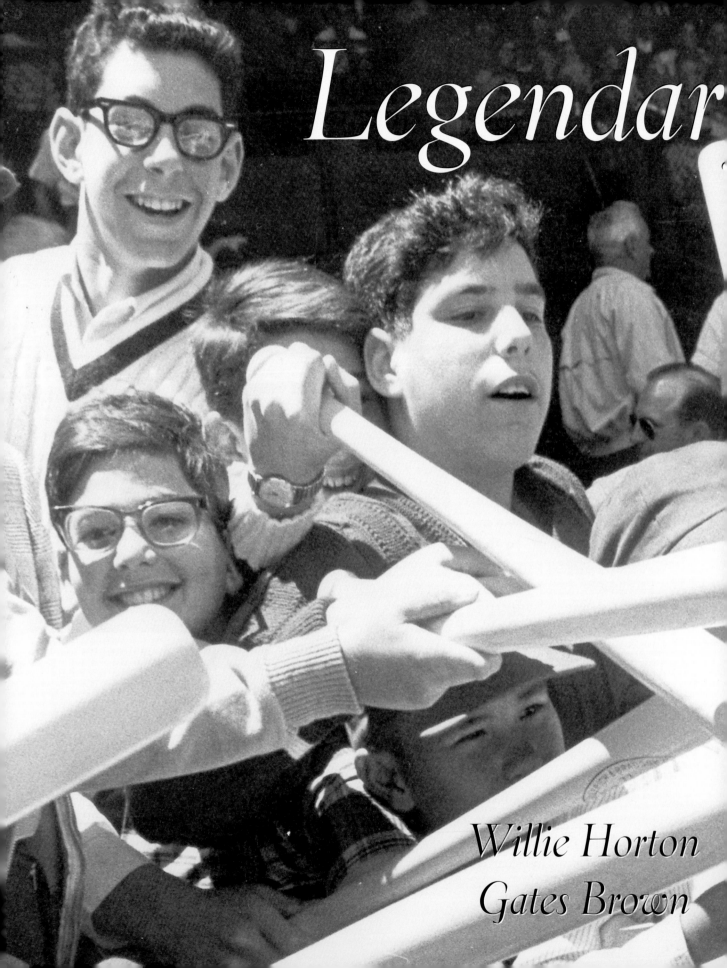

Legendar

Willie Horton
Gates Brown

Lumber

Heavy-hitting Willie Horton was always a fan favorite playing for his hometown team.

Charlie Maxwell   Heinie Manush

Norm Cash

Homegrown Horton was feared

By Mike O'Hara ✦ *The Detroit News*
ORIGINALLY PRINTED JUNE 2, 1985

H is new uniform has the pinstripes of the most famous team in baseball history — maybe the best known American sports franchise ever — and his home base is Yankee Stadium. He remembers Yankee Stadium when the monuments were at the base of the wall in center field. Now they've been moved in the redesigned stadium to a place called Memorial Park, behind the fence.

Somewhere Willie Horton keeps a monument of his own. It is a baseball uniform without pinstripes. On the front is an olde English D. On the back is his number 23, and above it, his name "HORTON".

It is the uniform he wore for the Detroit Tigers for 15 years, from 1963, when he started the season with them but was sent back to the minors as a confused young player who wasn't quite ready to handle major-league pitching and pressure, until Ralph Houk shipped him to Texas in 1977.

Gone, traded, shipped. All the words they use when somebody is moved from one team to another. You can add sent packing.

Except Detroit never left Willie Horton.

"I cried the day I left there," Horton said the other night from a spot on the bench on the home team's dugout at Yankee Stadium. "I've still got that uniform. They signed me when I was 17. They raised me. All I know is the Tigers."

Willie Horton is 42, and his home for the last seven years has been in Kirkland, Wash., a suburb of Seattle in the majestic Pacific Northwest, where he has come to love the mountains and the peaceful community.

But deep down, home to Horton is the heart of Detroit. It is where he starred in high school and on the sandlots. It is the drive up the Lodge Freeway to get to Michigan and Trumbull, where Tiger Stadium is a monument to a city's baseball team and its passion for those who graced it.

In a manner which many young athletes might not understand, Willie Horton and Detroit share the same heartbeat. They belong to each other, this city that embraces its heroes and anti-heroes. All Detroit ever asked of most of its athletes — especially those who sprouted from its soil — was that they punched in on time, worked their shift, and did their best.

Willie Horton did that.

His statistics are there to document his accomplishments in

> *"I cried the day I left there. I've still got that uniform. They signed me when I was 17. They raised me. All I know is the Tigers."*
>
> WILLIE HORTON

✦ ✦ ✦

Willie Horton hit 20-plus homers six times with Detroit.

the major leagues; 2,028 games played, 1,993 hits, 325 home runs.

But long ago, Horton already had made a mark on the town as perhaps no high school baseball player ever did.

It is not unusual for high school athletes to achieve celebrity status in Detroit, but most frequently they play basketball and football. Reggie Harding, Lonnie Sanders, Henry Carr — who ran track and played football — Ralph Simpson, Spencer Haywood and most recently Antoine Joubert, were young men who made their mark on the hardwood court or the football field.

But Horton did it in baseball. He was a legend on the sandlots, until the Tigers signed him in 1961 at the age of 17. He had a following. There was the time he hit a home run into the upper deck at Tiger Stadium in the City League's championship game. Once in a game at Northwestern Field, Horton launched a moon shot. The shortstop drift-

ed back and called for the ball, which continued to soar until it finally landed on Grand River, some 500 feet away. Or so that story goes. Who knows? The ball might have landed on the other side of Grand River.

He was Willie the Wonder as a young player with the Tigers. He could carry a team for a week with a hot streak. He made the old park crackle.

"I never realized how a person can control a city as a young man," he said. "I'm proud of that."

He got something in return this weekend. He came back to be honored last week at a testimonial dinner at Cobo Hall. Proceeds from the dinner are going to help establish an Afro-American Sports Hall of Fame Gallery in Detroit.

"I haven't been able to sleep," Horton said before leaving for Detroit. "I hope I can hold up. This puts the icing on some old scars."

One scar healed when he got back to the major leagues after an absence of more than seven years as a "tranquility coach" for the Yankees. He was hired by Billy Martin after Martin replaced Yogi Berra as manager after 10 games of the season.

Tranquility coach? It is something new to baseball. Or is it?

"They've had tranquility coaches in baseball before." Martin said, puffing — rather tranquilly — on his pipe. "They called them peacemakers, right?

"That's what he is. There was a tranquility gun in the west: the Colt."

Willie Horton, hired gun — peacemaker.

✦ ✦ ✦

131

Need a hit? Just call on Brown

By Jerry Green ✦ *The Detroit News*
ORIGINALLY PRINTED AUGUST 16, 1988

I t was the second day of the 1968 season and Gates Brown sat in the dugout at Tiger Stadium. He watched Denny McLain pitch. And as he did, Gates Brown steamed with anger.

Twenty years later, the circumstances are still fresh in his mind.

"You remember in '67, when I got hurt, broke my wrist, they brought up Lenny Green?" Brown said. "He did a good job for the Tigers. In '68, you know, hell, I was in the big leagues five years by then and they came to me the last couple of days before the end of spring training and they said, 'Gates, it's between you and Lenny, (and) you just made the team.'

"And it kind of ticked me off. I ain't got nothing against Lenny, but he was 38 and I'm 26. I can hit. I can. To think that I was that close. They could have been joking, I don't know.

"I always felt we'd have won in '67 if I hadn't been hurt. We lost by one game the last day. I thought I would have won one game for us during the summer.

Before that second game in 1968, Manager Mayo Smith said Brown was available — via trade or cash.

"I'd like another right-handed pinch hitter," Smith said. "We have plenty of left-handers."

So Brown stewed about the treatment.

Eddie Mathews was the first left-handed pinch hitter in that game against the Red Sox, batting for McLain in the seventh. Tom Matchick, the second left-handed pinch hitter, was used in the eighth.

The game remained tied into the home half of the ninth. Jon Warden, a rookie relief pitcher, was to be the lead-off batter. Smith sent out Brown to hit for Warden.

"I took the home run off John Wyatt in the ninth," Brown said. "We took off from there."

The Tigers beat the Red Sox 4-3. It was their first victory in '68. They would, in a few days, move into first place. They would win nine straight games.

But more than anything, Brown's pinch-hit home run started a pattern the Tigers would follow through the championship season. They would win in this melodramatic style all the way to the World Series. McLain's 30th victory in September would be of the last-licks variety. The pennant clincher a few nights later would be the same, on Don Wert's single in the bottom of the ninth.

Throughout the summer, Brown would provide the mighty punch with his speciality. He was the pinch hitter extraordinaire, finishing 16-for-26, a .577 average in the clutch.

A mid-August weekend series was especially memorable. The Red Sox were back at Tiger Stadium.

Brown got a pinch-hit home run in the first game, but the Tigers still lost.

Then, on Sunday, Aug. 11, the Tigers and Red Sox played a doubleheader. The first game dawdled into

✦ ✦ ✦

the 14th inning, four hours and 23 minutes. It was 4-4. Smith sent up Brown to bat for Mickey Lolich.

"That was a funny game," Brown recalled. "You try to guess along with the manager. I had myself hitting three or four or five times. It never materialized, until the 14th. And then it was two outs with nobody on. I really didn't think he'd use me then.

"But lady luck was with me. I hit a home run. I think that was one of my most memorable games."

Smith rewarded Brown by putting him in left field for the second game.

The Red Sox scored three runs in the top of the ninth and took a 5-2 lead. It was dark out. The lights were on. It was almost 9 when the bottom of the ninth began. Then the Tigers tied it with a quaint rally — a walk to Jim Price, Bill Freehan's bloop hit over the shortstop, Dick McAuliffe's dribbled single through the infield, Mickey Stanley's bouncing single over the pitcher's head. Al Kaline's bloop single off the end of his bat. Not a solid hit — but this was the bottom of the ninth and these were the '68 Tigers. They were full of miracles.

Now, with the score 5-5 and Stanley at third, Kaline on first, Brown was the batter.

"I never thought I'd hit in the ninth," Brown said. He thought Smith would pinch hit for the supreme pinch hitter because a left-hander was on the mound.

"Sparky Lyle was pitching, he had some good sliders," Brown said. "It was a breaking ball away from me. I didn't hit that good. The infield was in. I hit it

A pinch hitter extraordinaire, Gates Brown had his ups and downs with manager Mayo Smith.

between George Scott and the second baseman (Mike Andrews). Soon as I hit, I knew it was through if George couldn't get it — he was the best first baseman in the league — and if he couldn't get it, nobody could."

A squib single, Stanley scored, a four-run rally in the ninth, the Tigers won 6-5. Brown drove in the winning run in both games.

The tip-off for the kind of career Brown would have was his first major-league at bat against the Red Sox in 1963. He was a pinch hitter — and he hit a home run.

❖ ❖ ❖

133

Sunday no sabbath for Maxwell

By Bill Brennan ✦ *The Detroit News*
Originally printed July 5, 1981

Charlie Maxwell was noted for his dramatic Sunday punch, and after one such productive day with the Detroit Tigers, a waggish copy editor headlined Maxwell's efforts "Paw Paw Pow Pow."

Any Tiger fan of the mid-1950s through the early 1960s knew instantly what the headline meant: Maxwell, who had put the small grape-growing community of Paw Paw on the map of Michigan, had hit two home runs.

Maxwell, who still makes his home in Paw Paw and who today is as trim and fit as back when he played left field for the Boston Red Sox, Tigers and Chicago White Sox, shrugs off his talent for hitting Sunday homers "as one of the oddities of baseball."

"When I was with the Tigers, Frank Lary was my roommate, and the Yankees figured all Lary had to do was throw his glove on the mound to beat them. I remember the Tigers going into Yankee Stadium and Lary beating them — and then we went on to Kansas City and Lary pitched again and all they did was hit the darndest line drives off of him you ever saw. About the third or fourth inning Lary was advising the infielders to take out additional life insurance.

"But that's what makes baseball interesting, it's unpredictable."

Baseball may be unpredictable but Maxwell never was. And fans always knew the chances were good that old Paw Paw would hit a home run on Sunday — in a doubleheader against the Yankees. One Sunday in 1959 he hit four to tie the major league record.

Maxwell spent the last two years of his career with the White Sox and while there at the age of 38 he decided it was time to call it quits.

He always knew that when he had finished with the sport, he would return to Paw Paw, his hometown, a place where he has always taken an active role in community affairs.

"I did not want to be a hanger-on. I could have played for another year or two, but I always knew it had to end sometime, so I talked it over with my wife and decided to retire. We always knew we would return to Paw Paw."

The Maxwells had good reason to return there. They have a beautiful lakeside home. It was from an easy chair at the lake's edge that he reminisced about his years in baseball.

Maxwell remembers his first homer in the majors — also a grand slammer — off Satchel Paige.

"When I say that it makes me feel old, but they had a special on Satchel Paige the other night and that's what made me think of it."

Although Maxwell held the American League record for the most consecutive errorless games by an outfielder (194) set in 1957-58 and tied the American League season mark for highest fielding percentage by an outfielder (.997 in 1957), his fielding was also suspect.

"That went back to when I was with the Red Sox,"

✦ ✦ ✦

Maxwell says. "I was known as Ted Williams' caddy then. I'd go in for him as a defensive move. I never had a strong arm, but I had an accurate arm.

"They'd never run on me like they would on Rocky Colavito. He had a powerful arm, but one time he might throw a strike and the next the ball would be in the seats.

"We were playing the Yankees and I went in for Williams in the late innings. They had men on base and the ball came out to me and I fired it to second base, but nobody covered and the ball skipped away and everybody scored and we lost. I got the blame, but I made the right play. That's when it all started. They said I was a bad defensive player. It all boiled down to that one play."

Tiger fans have always had a great affection for Maxwell.

There was good reason for the fans' support. Besides his Sunday dramatics, Maxwell was a clutch hitter.

"The team used to keep statistics then on hits in the later innings," he recalls. "Hits that either tied or won games, and Bill Tuttle and I were 1-2. I think I led Tuttle by a point and I seldom hit into a double play. Fellows like Kaline, of courses, hit for better average."

Maxwell never had a desire to remain in baseball after his playing career.

"You are at the mercy of the owner when you are a manager.

"There are 26 teams in the majors, as a manager, you are at the mercy of 26 owners. It's not for me."

Opposing pitchers rarely had a prayer when Maxwell stepped to the plate on Sunday afternoons at Tiger Stadium.

◆ ◆ ◆

Cash homers were rooftop wonders

By Larry Middlemas ✦ *The Detroit News*
ORIGINAL PRINT DATE UNKNOWN

When Norm Cash hits a home run, the ball takes off with its little rabbit ears twitching and slams into the second or third deck. But when Charlie Dressen talks about home runs, he wonders why Cash doesn't hit some dinky ones.

You don't complain too hard about a guy who socks 25 or so homers a year (his 19th yesterday traveled about 400 feet), but Dressen wonders a little.

"Why doesn't he ever hit the fly ball that just drops into the seats?" Dressen was asking no one in particular before the Tigers started this road trip. "He hits the good home runs, but he should get some cheap ones.

"The trouble is he hits the ball hard to center field. If he'd pull it more, he wouldn't have to hit it so hard to get home runs."

Now there's a switch for you.

Back in 1961, when Cash won the American League batting championship, he pulled well, but hit in all directions.

So when he failed to come close to that .361 average again, one of the common comments was that he was trying to pull everything, trying only for home runs, instead of settling for hits and letting the homers come as they would.

Now we hear Dressen saying he could pull some more.

"I think I do pull as much as I can," Cash said. "I'm not thinking of pushing it to left just for hits, but sure, you hit to left if that's where the ball is pitched.

"I don't see all one kind of pitching. Each club pitches the way it thinks it can get you out, and they have different ideas.

"The main difference I notice in the last few years is that the pitchers don't challenge me as much. I mean they don't try to throw their best pitch past me. I don't see near as many good pitches as I used to."

It's an oddity of Tiger history that with one of the most inviting targets for left-handed home run hitters — the right field stands only 325 feet away along the foul line and no more than 360 in most of the home run range — Detroit never has had one of the greatest left-handed sluggers.

Cash and Charley Maxwell have been good. Cash hit 41 homers in 1961 and Maxwell hit 31 in 1959, but neither has had a lengthy slugging career. Vic Wertz was one of the better left-handed sluggers of his time, but spent only a small part of his career here.

Ty Cobb batted left-handed in setting baseball's career average of .367, but Cobb wasn't a power hitter. Neither, particularly, was Charlie Gehringer.

So those inviting right field seats never have been as valuable as the short right fields in Yankee Stadium or the Polo Grounds, for example.

✦ ✦ ✦

Cash has 12 homers at home this season, four to the third deck and four to the second. Most of his four to the lower deck were out toward right center, to flies toward the short target.

As Dressen says, he doesn't give himself a shot at accidental home runs by hitting flies to right.

In fact, in Detroit's 127 games, does anyone want to guess how many times Cash had flied to the right fielder? Sixty? Forty-five?

The answer is 16 times, an average of less than once a week.

But after Dressen's comment about wasting his power in center field, you'd expect more flies out there. He has hit only 26. He even has 25 flies to left field.

Look back again, and the scorebook shows he has 90 infielder grounders.

There's nothing wrong with hitting the ball on the ground; lots of that kind go through for hits. But a man hitting grounders and low line drives is not going to bloop many cheap home runs.

This isn't meant to suggest remedies. That's the manager's problem. But anyway, that's where much of the old Cash power has gone.

Meanwhile, when he catches hold of one, it sure doesn't leave much doubt.

Slugging Norm Cash hit more homers out of Tiger Stadium than any other Tigers player.

❖ ❖ ❖

Manush won batting title in 1926

By Larry Middlemas ✦ *The Detroit News*
ORIGINALLY PRINTED APRIL 12, 1964

"**G**lad to see you," the big, white haired man greeted the visitor to the house on 7th Street. "I'm Heinie Manush." The old Tiger batting star was wearing slacks and a white shirt, open at the throat as he sat on the front porch.

In another hour he'd have to put on a coat and tie and fly to New York to appear on a TV show.

This is the year that everyone is remembering Heinie Manush. He was voted into baseball's Hall of Fame in February and will be installed on July 27, a week to the day after his 63rd birthday.

"I had some honors in my career," he recalled. "I wanted to win a batting championship and I did.

"In 1929 a friend of mine had tickets for the World Series in Chicago and I turned down going along with him. I said I didn't want to see the Series until I played in it. Four years later I did play in the World Series.

"But nothing can compare with being elected to the Hall of Fame while you're alive and can appreciate it.

"I wish Harry Heilmann could have lived to enjoy it.

"Harry was a great one. If he'd had Ty Cobb's temperament he might have been as great as any ball player ever."

Manush who won his batting title with a .378 average in 1926, will be in Detroit May 7 as a guest of honor at the Capuchin dinner, and he said he's looking forward to it.

HENRY EMMET MANUSH
1923–1939
SLUGGING OUTFIELDER
FOR 6 MAJOR LEAGUE CLUBS. BATTING
CHAMPION OF A.L. AT .378 WITH 1926 TIGERS.
LIFETIME AVERAGE OF .330 IN 2,009
MAJOR LEAGUE GAMES. HAD 2,524 HITS.

"I haven't been there since I was a coach with Washington in '53 and '54," he said, "I'll be in early enough to see the Tigers play the Red Sox. I'd like to see John Pesky (Boston manager). I was his manager when he played his first game."

Manush said he watches Saturday and Sunday major-league games on TV and goes to some spring exhibitions in Sarasota, where the White Sox train. Detroit and Washington, his old clubs, are his favorites.

"But it's not the same when you don't know the players any more." he admitted. "I talk with some of the managers and coaches. They're the ones I know."

He no longer has any baseball connection.

"I did some scouting for Washington a couple of years ago, but that's an awful job." said Manush, a major leaguer from 1923 to 1938. "Sleep and eat and travel. You never get a chance to exercise."

He does his hitting on the golf course now.

"I try to play nine holes every day." Manush said. "Do you play golf?"

His visitor had stopped on his way to a par three course.

✦ ✦ ✦

Manush gave up plumbing for a baseball career.

"I don't like to play there," Manush said.

"Sure, but you're a hitter."

"No," he said. "I just don't like driving off those rubber mats instead of regular tees.

"I played my first round of golf at Oakland Hills in Detroit about 1923. That's a great place to start. I must have shot 200.

"I came to Sarasota in 1935, when there were only about 3,500 people. But there were some other ball players who were good golfers, and I decided I'd be a good golfer, too.

"I hit left-handed, of course, and I'd hit that big sweeping slice. Jimmy Thompson, the pro told me once there was no name for the kind of drives I hit."

Old friends, but not old ball players, are the competition now.

"There are only a couple of others here all year," he said. "Do you remember Billy Sullivan, the catcher who was with the Tigers for a while? He's in business here. I see him at church. I have played with Paul Waner, but he's been pretty sick lately. He still hits the ball straight, with that beautiful swing, but only about 150 yards."

Manush has three daughters and seven grandchildren. A daughter in Sarasota and her family will go along when he is installed formally in the Hall of Fame this summer and attends the annual exhibition game at Cooperstown, N.Y.

"It will make a nice trip for them." he said. "You'll fly to New York and then go to Utica, and I think a bus meets us there. I've never been to Cooperstown. "

After Manush won the American League batting championship in 1926 with a .378 average, he was traded the next year to the St. Louis Browns. Manush hit .378 again for the Browns in 1928, moved on to several other clubs and wound up a 17-year career in 1939 with a .330 lifetime average.

When he batted .342 one season for the Washington Senators, they cut his pay the next year.

A big, strong boy from Alabama, Manush started out to be a plumber's helper until he decided he could make almost as much money playing baseball. He joined the Tigers in 1923 and batted his way into an outfield with Cobb, Harry Heilmann and sometimes Bob Fothergill.

✦ ✦ ✦

Everyone was a Rudy York fan when he
hit 18 home runs during August 1937.

Cecil Fielder   Schoolboy Rowe   Rudy

Fantastic Feats

Fielder put bash back into baseball

By Bob Wojnowski ✦ *The Detroit News*
ORIGINALLY PRINTED AUGUST 15, 1994

Vince Coleman throws a firecracker. Bret Saberhagen throws bleach. Pitchers throw beanballs and hitters throw tantrums. The national pastime is stuck in the muck, spinning its tires, and mud flying everywhere, landing on everyone.

Cecil Fielder shakes his head. He searches for the words, not sure what to say, only sure something should be said.

"I don't understand it," he finally says. "Any time you see something on TV about baseball, it's bad. There's a lot of good in the game, there really is. There are a lot of people trying to respect the game, trying to be good people. You just have to look for them."

Before things get any messier, it's time to look at Cecil. If we condemn the Colemans and the characters who leave dirty fingerprints on the game, we must celebrate Cecil, who leaves imprints that will last much longer.

The closer we look, the more we realize what we've missed. Overlooking consistent greatness is the easiest thing to do, which is why we do it.

If he hangs on to his slender advantage, Fielder will lead the major leagues in RBI for the fourth consecutive season, an unprecedented feat (he had 97 to 96 for Chicago's Frank Thomas). Arguably, it would become one of baseball's untouchable records. Babe Ruth's mark of three consecutive RBI titles (1919-21) stood a mere 71 years until Cecil came along.

In three-plus seasons with the Tigers, Fielder has been a power hitter of historic proportions, with home-run totals of 51, 44 and 35, and RBI totals of 132, 133 and 124. Yet he has started in the All-Star game only once, and never been the league MVP.

All of which begs the questions: Do we realize what we're witnessing? Do we understand it? Do we appreciate it?

It is easy for sustained excellence to slide to the side, a steady hum drowned by the clatter of the daily police blotter, or by the clamor of a singularly remarkable quest, such as John Olerud's pursuit of .400. It is easier when the man performing the feats is a quiet hulk, an ordinary perpetrator of extraordinary deeds, a man determined to remain that way.

Fielder is the rare ballplayer still defined by what he does on the field, nothing more. In ballparks and press boxes, in newsrooms and living rooms, people stop when the big guy lumbers to the plate. It is the way it used to be for great players, before endorsement and appearances and barroom antics. It is the simple little formula the game lost as it has grown.

"Believe me, I like things just the way they are," Fielder says. "I like to be able to go home and be with my wife, be with the kids, talk to my neighbors' kids. That's enough for me. That's more than enough for me."

It did not used to be enough. In his first two seasons

Cecil Fielder, taking a walk on the left-field roof at Tiger Stadium in 1993, is the only Tiger to hit 25-plus homers in seven straight seasons.

in Detroit, Fielder wanted it all. After he finished second in MVP voting to Rickey Henderson in 1990 and to Cal Ripken Jr. in 1991, he fumed. Perhaps people looked to his size and figured it was easy to do what he did. Perhaps he finished where he deserved to finish, because the MVP award recognizes the best season, not the best two seasons.

It was difficult because Fielder knew more than everyone else. He knew how far he'd come, from Japan, from baseball oblivion. He knew he'd done it the hard way, the humbling way, up the back staircase. In baseball, it seems, that's the wrong way, if recognition is what you crave.

"I admit, I was somewhat bitter toward the game then," Fielder says. "I talked to my wife after the second MVP vote and she helped me get through it because I was really upset. Then I just thought, What does it really matter? What does it mean?

"I got thrown out of baseball and came back and showed I could play, that's enough for me. All the negative people who said I couldn't play, they got lost. They couldn't say, 'I told you so.' That's what motivates me now. I don't want anybody to ever say 'I told you so'."

So he says he has stopped worrying about MVP awards. He probably won't win it this year either, not with Olerud flirting with .400.

That's why there would be sweet retribution in the RBI crown. If he wins it, he won't need a vote to take his spot in the books.

◆ ◆ ◆

Rowe had talent, head and heart

By Sam Greene ✦ *The Detroit News*
ORIGINALLY PRINTED JANUARY 9, 1961

Schoolboy Rowe had all the attributes of a great pitcher — size and strength, head and heart.

At his peak he had an overpowering fast ball, a quick breaking curve and a change of pace that a contemporary described as "magic." In addition to his towering skill, Rowe had that indefinable quality known as "color." Winning or losing, he had a dramatic flair rooted in a commanding presence.

Rowe ranks at or near the top of the all-time list of Detroit pitchers. Surely, he deserves to be bracketed with Wild Bill Donovan and George Mullin of the old days; Tommy Bridges, his teammate on three-pennant winning teams, and Harold Newhouser, the left-handed ace of the middle 1940s.

Rowe was proud of two records. Both were set in 1934 when Mickey Cochrane drove the Tigers to their first pennant in 25 years.

In the regular season, Rowe won 16 straight games for an American League mark shared by Walter Johnson of Washington (1912), and Robert (Lefty) Grove of Philadelphia (1931).

Then in the World Series with the St. Louis Cardinals, the Schoolboy retired 22 straight batters while winning the 12-inning second game in a duel with Paul Dean. That was a World Series record that stood until Don Larsen of the New York Yankees pitched a perfect game against the Brooklyn Dodgers in 1956.

Rowe had a flair for drama and a relaxed attitude off the mound.

Rowe was only in his second season with the Tigers when he joined three pitching immortals with 16 straight victories. The streak reached its climax in Washington on Aug. 25, 1934.

Going into the ninth inning, it looked as if Rowe at last would be beaten. The Tigers were behind 2-1, but Hank Greenberg produced by driving a pitch by Monte Weaver over the right field fence.

After Marvin Owen singled, Weaver was replaced by Jack Russell. A single by Pete Fox sent Owen to

✦ ✦ ✦

144

third and brought Rowe to the plate for what proved a decisive thrust.

Rowe fouled off two pitches before he hit a short fly into left field for a single that scored Owen and put the Tigers ahead. Fox added an insurance run when Pete Susko, the Washington first baseman, made a wild throw off Jo Jo White's grounder.

Rowe still had to retire the Senators in the ninth to preserve his 16th straight victory. He did it despite a low throw by shortstop Bill Rogell that enabled Fred Schulte, the leadoff batter, to reach first base.

After Schulte advanced on an infield out, Rowe struck out two pinch-hitters — Dave Harris and Cecil Travis — to assure himself a share in a rare record. His attempt to extend it failed in the next series at Philadelphia where a triple by outfielder Bing Miller, afterward a Detroit coach, was the big hit in a defeat for the Schoolboy.

Schoolboy Rowe's 16-game winning streak in 1934 tied an American League record at the time.

After helping Detroit win successive pennants in 1934-35, Rowe was plagued from time to time by arm trouble. In 1938, the Tigers sent him to their Beaumont farm in the belief that the Texas sun would prove beneficial.

The skeptics thought the Schoolboy never again would pitch in the major leagues, but he fooled them. He returned to the Tigers in 1939 and stayed four seasons. When they won the pennant in 1940, Rowe turned in 26 victories against three losses.

Two years later the Tigers sold Rowe to Brooklyn, but he did not tarry long with the Dodgers. They shipped him to Montreal and again the skeptics shouted that the majors had seen the last of the Schoolboy.

But Rowe bounced back with the Philadelphia Phillies and compiled a 14-8 record in 1943. His career then was interrupted by two years in the Navy for World War II.

After the war Rowe returned to the Phillies and remained until 1949 when he asked for his release to accept a job in the Detroit farm system.

"That's where I made a big mistake," Rowe once said. "The Phillies won the pennant the next year. So it turned out that I talked myself out of a World Series cut."

In the last 10 years Rowe had varied jobs with the Tigers. He managed the Williamsport, Pa., affiliate in the Eastern League and served as a roving coach of the farm system before coming to Briggs Stadium as pitching coach for 1954-55.

◆ ◆ ◆

Home run record outlived York

By Watson Spoelstra ✦ *The Detroit News*
ORIGINALLY PRINTED FEBRUARY 6, 1970

Rudolph Preston York was an uncomplicated stylist as a power hitter for the Detroit Tigers. York, who set a major-league record when he hit 18 home runs in a month as a rookie, once said: "I just shut my eyes and swing."

The powerful York had a smooth swing, and most baseball men considered him a smart hitter.

When he broke in with the Tigers in the late 30s, York was a 210-pounder described as equipped with "shoulders of a wrestler, wrists of a blacksmith and the native shrewdness of a Dizzy Dean."

York was of German-Irish-Indian extraction, and he became an exciting player in Detroit when Mickey Cochrane was the manager.

In 1937, his rookie year, York hit 35 home runs in 104 games, roughly two-thirds of the schedule. He would never hit that many again, twice hitting 34.

Babe Ruth had knocked 17 home runs in September while establishing his record of 60 in 1927.

York surpassed this feat by having the hottest month the game has ever known.

Rudy did it the hard way. On the last day of the month he drove two over the fence at Navin Field in a victory over Washington. The victim was Pete Appleton, a University of Michigan product.

The problem with York was finding a place for him to play. The Tigers tried him at third base, left field and catcher before shifting Hank Greenberg to the outfield in 1940 to make room for York at first base.

York started poorly at first base, but after a few

York played in four all-star games and finished his 12-year American League career with Chicago and Philadelphia with a .275 batting average, 277 home runs and 1,152 runs batted in.

adjustments he developed into one of the better glove men of his time. In two years, York had improved his fielding enough to break the American League record for assists by a first baseman with 146.

Besides, the Greenberg switch paid off. Detroit won the 1940 pennant under Del Baker with Greenberg in left field, York at first base and Birdie Tebbetts behind the plate as York's successor.

Rudy made the World Series twice with Detroit, in 1940 and 1945. The Tigers traded him to Boston in a deal for shortstop Eddie Lake, and Rudy promptly got into the World Series again with the Red Sox in 1946.

York played in four all-star games and finished his 12-year American League career with Chicago and Philadelphia with a .275 batting average, 277 home runs and 1,152 runs batted in.

✦ ✦ ✦

146

York's 18-homer month showed his power

As baseball statistics are commonly computed by the game, week and season, there may be the first impulse to depreciate Rudy York's feat of hitting 18 home runs in one month.

In our judgment, the record and the manner of its making are pretty hot stuff. It was not one of those cases where a record is broken, and someone discovers it later by checking the book.

York knew Tuesday he had one game in which to tie or beat Ruth's record. We do not pretend to know the workings of the York mind, but it would appear obvious that he took the Tuesday game in stride, and that the setting of a record was incidental to the day's work.

There is a criterion of baseball's changing values in the fact that York, with 30 home runs, is one ahead of Ruth's seasonal mark in 1919, which led to his purchase by the Yankees for $125,000.

While changes in the ball and in the major league parks obviate a fair comparison of the two men. York's new record speaks for itself. He has not been tested by a full season of major league pitching, but his August achievement is a fairly conclusive proof of extraordinary power. During the month he faced all kinds of pitching, and he continued to bust 'em over the fence.

Rudy York's record of 18 August home runs included 12 in the last 14 games.

♦ ♦ ♦

147

Crawford was baseball's triple threat

By H.G. Salsinger ✦ *The Detroit News*
ORIGINALLY PRINTED FEBRUARY 5, 1957

S am Crawford was born 50 years too soon. He was equipped for the post-1920 era of baseball rather than the pre-1920 span. He belonged to the power age. The so-called "dead" ball made it impossible for him to capitalize on his muscular talents.

During his 18-year career in the majors, he hit 312 triples and no player since his time has come close to matching his record.

It was one of the few that Ty Cobb could not reach. The best Cobb could do in 24 years of big league competition was 297, the second highest total. Honus Wagner's 250 triples is the National League's all-time high.

Crawford's record will last as long as the lively ball. Three-base hits have gone out of style. No player in the American League hit more than 11 last year, and four players were tied at 11. Bill Bruton of Milwaukee led the National League with 15.

The leading sluggers of the lively-ball decades go for the distance and not three-quarters of the distance. Babe Ruth hit 714 home runs and 136 triples. Lou Gehrig racked up 493 home runs and 161 triples. Jimmy Foxx's record shows 534 home runs and 125 triples. Hank Greenberg hit 331 home runs, 71 triples. Hack Wilson collected 244 home runs, 67 triples.

Crawford hit 95 home runs and 312 triples. The present ball, propelled by the same power, travels at least 50 feet farther than the "dead" ball.

Not all of Crawford's triples would have been home

runs, but many flies were caught off his bat that would have landed in the stands today.

When Philadelphia played Detroit, Connie Mack instructed his pitchers to pitch to Crawford's strength.

Sam was a lefthanded pull hitter, and right field at Navin Field was some 40 feet deeper than it is today. There was no pavilion in right field.

Mr. Mack would station Danny Murphy, his right fielder, against the wall and his pitchers would throw fast balls inside to Crawford. In one game Murphy caught five flies off Crawford's bat, all within 10 or 15 feet of the wall.

No pitcher would dare to pitch fast balls to Crawford today.

Crawford, like Perry Como, was a barber by trade. He was born in Wahoo, Neb., and from his birthplace stemmed his nickname, "Wahoo Sam." He spent only one season in the minors, making his major league debut with Cincinnati in 1899. He was six feet tall and weighed just under 200.

Not noted for foot speed, he still succeeded in steal-

✦ ✦ ✦

One of the greatest 'dead ball' era players, Crawford collected a record 312 triples.

ing 367 bases. He stole 41 in 1912 which is more than the distance hitters of today will steal in their entire careers, for stolen bases, like the three-base hit, have gone out of style.

As his fame spread, the residents of Wahoo erected a huge sign at the city limits: "This is Wahoo, Neb., Home of Sam Crawford."

Years later Sam must have often thought of the sign and reflected on the shallowness of baseball fame since fortune turned against him after his retirement.

Crawford's last season with the Tigers was 1917. He played four more years in the Pacific Coast League.

Sam invested his savings in a pecan grove, but the depression of the early 1930s wiped him out. In 1935 he turned to umpiring and served four years in the Pacific Coast League. He quit calling 'em as he saw 'em explaining : "I can't endure night baseball."

A few years ago when he visited Detroit he was invited to attend a night game at Briggs Stadium. He refused, saying he wanted no part of baseball under artificial light.

♦ ♦ ♦

LeFlore's effort overshadowed past

By Jerry Green ✦ *The Detroit News*
ORIGINALLY PRINTED MAY 26, 1976

He is Ron LeFlore, a professional ballplayer. He is nothing more, nothing less. It took a heroic batting streak and a .400 average to make him that. Other men become professional ballplayers the day they sign the contracts and deposit the checks in the bank.

But, Ronnie LeFlore was imprisoned by the burden of his past.

Now in late May of his third season with the Detroit Tigers there is genuine acclaim. He is the leading batter in the big leagues. He has hit successfully in 27 consecutive games. The streak is the longest in the American League in a quarter century.

LeFlore has become a big leaguer with a present and a future.

"My past shouldn't matter any more," LeFlore said. "I prefer that people talk about my baseball ability. Even in Boston the other night a reporter asked me why I went to prison."

His sentence continued after he was freed from Jackson. The Tigers rushed him through the farm system and brought him to the major leagues in less than a year. They thought of him as a curiosity and reasoned that people would pay to see him play.

Rookies brought to the majors in August of a failing season do not generate much publicity. Ron LeFlore's life story made a juicy subject in the national magazines. He was an ex-con with an engaging personality and he disclosed the truth about himself. *Time* magazine did an article on him beneath the heading: "A batter from the pen."

Now he's just "A batter."

"I'm glad I'm getting ink now because I'm playing baseball," LeFlore said yesterday, "not because I went to prison. I'm trying to be accepted as a ballplayer. I think I've done a pretty good job of it.

"But it was tough. Every time I turned around somebody came up to me to ask about my past. It was the same question every day. About prison."

He is a professional ballplayer, nothing else now, and he had strong pride. I figured he might be reassigned to the minors this year for additional seasoning. Ralph Houk, the manager, might have thought of it, too. Houk started the season with another center fielder and LeFlore sulked through the first three games.

"I was very angry about it," he said. "I was the center fielder last year. I figured I didn't have a very good year last year. Then I looked it up and found half the center fielders hit under .258, my average.

"I thought I should have been in center field when the season started. Why should I not be in center field because I had a bad second half of the season? The whole team had a bad year. We lost 102 games. I didn't lose all 102.

"As a rookie, I played as good as anybody. I felt I was the fastest guy on the team. I didn't see a leadoff hitter on the team who could do what I could. The leadoff hitter is supposed to get on base. I did."

✦ ✦ ✦

Ron LeFlore led the Tigers in stolen bases six straight seasons.

He is a professional ballplayer only now — and he may gripe about the mistaken notions of the manager.

Whatever the reason, Houk's benching of LeFlore at the start of the season became a psychological prod. LeFlore's hitting streak began his first day in the batting order.

"Because I didn't play at the beginning of the year probably was better for me than if I'd been sent back to the minor leagues," LeFlore said.

"Last year I was pulling my head back," he said. "This year I'm just watching the ball and meeting it with the bat.

"I'm not saying I can go at the pace I am. But the points you pick up early in the year help if you go in a little slump.

"Fame is only momentary, with you one day and gone the next. That's what they say."

He is Ron LeFlore, a professional ballplayer. Nothing more, nothing less.

◆ ◆ ◆

Chan
Cali

Lance Parrish   *Goose Goslin*   *Willie H*

pionship
er

andez   Mickey Stanley   Lou Whitaker

Parrish put muscle into his position

By Tom Gage ✦ *The Detroit News*
Originally printed April 3, 1984

His rise to prominence was as quiet as his own hulking presence. It's almost as if the dust cleared one day and Lance Parrish had become the best catcher.

"That's how it was bound to happen," said Tigers' Manager Sparky Anderson. "Some guys burst upon the scene. Others improve every year and suddenly everybody notices. I think he's the best, or at least I can say this: I wouldn't trade him for anyone else."

There are louder catchers than Parrish.

He isn't as noisy as Baltimore's Rick Dempsey. Or as wily or experienced as Carlton Fisk.

Gary Carter gets more headlines and Tony Pena is better paid. But Parrish blends the most brawn, potential, muscle and raw talent.

He used to be Parrish, the hitter. He chased a lot of bad pitches, sliders mostly. But his production didn't suffer, unless one considers 24 home runs and 86 RBI in his second season for Detroit suffering.

Defense was a different story entirely. Still more potential than production. One season went by, two, and Parrish would say the same thing in October. He'd be happy with his hitting but the glove needed work.

"A lot of people called me lazy," he said. "It wasn't laziness. I didn't assert myself as much as some others do. That's not my style, telling people what to do right away. You have to give people reasons to listen to you."

So he did.

Size alone should be enough for most people to pay attention. With the torso of a bodybuilder, Parrish is a wall behind the plate. He got that way with years of weight-lifting — so many years and so much concern for his own biceps, in fact, that Anderson began to worry.

"I've seen guys get muscle bound before," said Sparky. "They end up being able to do little else than lift those barbells. I didn't want that happening."

One spring, Sparky said no to Parrish. He took away his weights.

"He knows it turned out for the best. All I wanted was the moderation he shows now," Anderson said. "As good as he can be, I didn't want him to mess himself up."

In his quiet way, there are few players who work harder or spend longer hours at the office than Parrish. Invariably, he is the last to leave the clubhouse — whether it be after a spring training practice or a twi-night doubleheader in July.

"When I came to Detroit, I could tell he was a player who could have it all if he wanted it," Anderson continued. "And that's where 'if' becomes a mighty big word.

"I've seen other players with potential who didn't go anywhere. They didn't want it badly enough, didn't sacrifice. It comes down to one word — dedication. Without it, even the best projects are back in the pack."

✦ ✦ ✦

154

Lance Parrish, not Kirk Gibson, led the Tigers in home runs in 1984.

From the time the Tigers signed Parrish out of Walnut High in California, he was targeted as a can't miss prospect, depending on the degree of that one intangible — dedication.

Baseball wasn't his only sport in high school, nor catcher his only position. Parrish could have gone to UCLA on a football scholarship after achieving high school All-America status, but he preferred baseball. Besides, he liked third base too much to switch.

Parrish caught his first two years in high school, but signed with the Tigers after a senior year as a third baseman. He didn't return to behind the plate until 1975 at Lakeland.

"When we drafted him (first in the 1974 draft) we considered him a catcher," said Bill Lajoie, now the Tigers general manager. "The spot was already filled on our team in the rookie league, so we kept him at third for awhile.

"He did all right. He stopped enough grounders down

there, but his future was catching. We always knew that."

Two years after the switch, Parrish was in the major leagues breaking in on a part-time basis for the Tigers in 1977. In 1979, he became the team's daily catcher.

In his own words, his talent was still "raw."

"I was on the right track by then, but hadn't been for long," he said. "As a catcher, I didn't know what I was doing until I went to Evansville in '77 and played for Les Moss. He was the first one who really helped me."

Moss, a former major league catcher, was Parrish's mechanic. He fixed most of the mistakes in Parrish's style — and no one was happier to see Moss named as Tiger manager in 1976 than Parrish.

"It meant a lot to me. I knew we'd continue to work together. And at that stage of my career, I needed it."

Moss didn't last long as the Tigers manager — but Parrish's career already was heading in the right direction.

"Let's just say I became aware of the things I had to do," he said.

Such as learning how to handle pitchers. At first, Parrish thought they would handle themselves.

"I felt they had a job to do and probably knew it. Who was I to tell them how to do their job?"

Even now, Parrish says: "I'd rather have them be confident in themselves than about me and the pitches I call. I'd rather have them shake me off."

Two years ago, the Tigers put Parrish in a rather dubious spotlight by taking the responsibility of calling pitches away from him. Roger Craig, the pitching coach, would give the sign from the dugout and Parrish would relay it to the mound.

"It wasn't anything against him," said Anderson. "Eventually, I think he learned from it."

Jack Morris, the Tigers' 20-game winner, agrees. "Lance is smarter behind the plate now," Morris said. "He calls a much better game than he used to."

◆ ◆ ◆

Goslin brought attitude, then a title

By H.G. Salsinger ◆ *The Detroit News*
ORIGINAL PRINT DATE UNKNOWN

When Mickey Cochrane signed on as manager of the Tigers in 1934 he knew the team needed an infusion of attitude if Detroit was expected to rise above its second-division status.

He decided that Leon "Goose" Goslin would best suit his purposes. Goslin had played on three pennant-winning teams, he had a first-division complex, he was aggressive and the ideal type.

The deal was made and it proved a very fortunate one for Cochrane and Detroit. It proved extremely fortunate for Goslin too. He had returned to Washington from St. Louis just in time to help Washington win another pennant and then he arrived in Detroit in time for another championship. Once more Goslin was on a team that landed in front while his teammates of the previous year finished in seventh place.

Goslin is of the slugger cast.

His type of batter is the type pitchers fear.

He is most dangerous in a pinch, when there are runners on the bases and when a hit means winning a ball game.

He hits a ball hard and drives it a long way quite frequently.

He is spending his fourteenth season in the American League and he had a lifetime batting average of .322 to show for these seasons.

He has always been a popular player. There are few games at Navin Field where the refrain "Yeah, Goose" is not shouted from the pavilions and bleachers. He was nicknamed "Goose" not because of any physical

Goose Goslin was a clutch hitter and one of the key ingredients on the Tigers' 1935 Series winner.

characteristics but because of his family name, the populace associating Goslin with gosling and his nickname was a natural outcrop.

He is not a great fielder but a good one. He is slow-

Goslin was always accommodating to his adoring Detroit fans.

er than he was, naturally, but he will tell you so and that is not natural for a ball player; each believes himself as fast as he was four and five years ago.

As Goslin's speed decreased, his judgment increased and discounted his loss of speed.

He has an excellent throwing arm, but a half dozen years ago he could not throw a ball 60 feet. His arm suddenly collapsed.

It "went dead," as Charlie Gehringer's did some years back.

But he was hitting so well that Stanley Harris, then manager of Washington, would not take him out of the lineup; he felt that a Goslin who could not throw 50 feet was still more valuable than another outfielder who could throw 500. So the shortstop or the third baseman would run out into left field on any ball hit to Goslin. He would toss it underhand and the infielder would relay it to the infield. That is how they went along.

Goslin tried to change himself into a left handed thrower. Other ball players have done that. Eddie Rousch, one of the best National League outfielders, accomplished the switch, but Goslin could not. He went to Atlantic City and rested in the sun. His arm finally returned, and he has had no trouble throwing a ball since that time.

He has been a bachelor all his life and is the only member of the Detroit team who rooms alone. He becomes nervous when he shares a room with someone else. Ball players say that is his only idiosyncrasy.

✦ ✦ ✦

Hernandez was MVP of '84 season

By Joe Falls ✦ *The Detroit News*
ORIGINALLY PRINTED FEBRUARY 19, 1990

Where does Willie Hernandez fit into the history of the Detroit Tigers? Hard to say. He was the man who brought this town the 1984 world championship — he more than Kirk Gibson, Alan Trammell, Lou Whitaker, Jack Morris and all the rest—but the announcement on Saturday night that he was no longer a member of the Tigers hardly caused a ripple of reaction.

Is that the ultimate impression he made on us? Is it goodbye and good riddance? Or is 1984 already ancient history around here?

We saw this happen with the '68 champion — how many forgot Denny and Willie and Norm and Gates and Al and Mickey when the '84 champions came along, and now here we are at the start of the 1990s, and the '84 champions also seem to be fading from memory. Only five remain — Jack Morris, Dave Bergman, Alan Trammell, Lou Whitaker and Chet Lemon.

Maybe that's how it goes, but whether you liked him or not, Willie Hernandez was one of the most colorful performers our town has ever had.

I do not mean to be disrespectful by calling him "Willie" instead of "Guillermo" but now that he is gone to play for the Oakland A's Triple-A team in Tacoma, I feel I can do this, because it was as Willie Hernandez that he brought us all the excitement — all that electricity — in that remarkable 1984 season.

What set him apart from most players on the Tigers is that he touched us all whenever he came in to pitch.

You always felt something stir within you whenever he was heading to the mound.

It could be good or it could be bad, but no one could ever ignore Willie Hernandez's presence in a baseball game.

Some would cheer and some would boo, but we all wondered what he was going to do. He could get them out with that sinking screwball, bending it like a pretzel, or he might groove a fastball and it would wind up bouncing around in the upper deck for another shattering loss.

You just never knew what was going to happen...and this was the essence of Willie Hernandez in Detroit.

He was a man who reached us every time he performed...you could not be lukewarm about him...and I am going to miss him.

✦ ✦ ✦

Willie Hernandez got the final out of the 1984 World Series and celebrated with catcher Lance Parrish.

✦ ✦ ✦

Stanley stars as long-shot shortstop

By Jerry Green ✦ *The Detroit News*
ORIGINAL PRINT DATE UNKNOWN

Amid the jubilation of the Tigers' pennant clinching in 1968, there was a shred of mystery. Mayo Smith had been a magician with his ball club since April.

But now, in September with the pennant won, Mayo would need more than the supernatural to figure how to play four outfielders in three positions in the World Series.

He had Mickey Stanley, the swiftest, surest center fielder in the league. He had Willie Horton and his smoking bat in left. And he had Jim Northrup, the grand slam artist, in right and also capable in center.

But it could not be a proper World Series without Al Kaline, the team's best player and club elder. Kaline had broken bones in his hand in June. He was healed and ready. As a pinch hitter reaching base, he had scored the runs that won Denny McLain's victory No. 30 and the pennant clincher. He must play right field in the World Series.

Mayo Smith called Mickey Stanley to a meeting.

"I still remember it just like it was yesterday," Stanley recalled two decades later. "It was about 10 days before the season was over. He called me up to his room in Baltimore and said: 'I want you to play shortstop.' I said, 'What?' Of course, I knew why, because every day I'd get to the park early and I'd get a pitcher or a coach or somebody to hit me ground balls to shortstop to wear off some nervous energy. So he had seen me field a lot of ground balls, and I'd find somebody to take the throws at first base.

"So he said: 'You're our shortstop.' And I said, 'Are you kidding?' My biggest concern was that I didn't mind

Mickey Stanley's Series debut at shortstop was an errorless success.

doing it, but I was afraid I'd let down the other guys. I wasn't concerned for myself, embarrassing myself, as much as costing the other guys a winning share of the

✦ ✦ ✦

160

World Series. He said: 'No, you're going to play the last six games of the regular season at shortstop and you're gonna be my shortstop in the World Series.'"

Immediately upon announcing his drastic gambit, Mayo Smith was deluged with criticism. Kaline had to be in the World Series against the Cardinals. Smith had a tough dilemma. But the manner in which he intended to resolve it was considered the boldest gamble a manager had ever made in a World Series. Stanley had never played shortstop before. Ray Oyler, a light hitter and a sweet fielder, had been the shortstop most of '68.

"Ray Oyler — he was the one who got left out — came over and wished me luck," Stanley said. "It showed an awful lot of class.

"I had a feeling a few of the other players were skeptical, but nobody really made any derogatory comments. Of course, nobody on that team did anyway. We had a bunch of real mature guys."

For days before the World Series, Smith had to explain and defend his daring move over and over. Stanley turned the long-debated confrontation between Denny McLain and Bob Gibson into a secondary story.

"It worked," said Stanley. "Kaline got a few hits and I didn't hurt us in the field. He brought Oyler in a few games when we were ahead in the seventh inning and threw me back in center, put Northrup in left and took Horton out of the game.

"I felt if he had enough confidence, he was in a hotter seat than I was."

The Cardinals, of course, were a speed team – Lou Brock, Curt Flood, Julian Javier down the lineup. They could punch the ball and they like to run. They would

Stanley was the league's top center fielder in 1968.

put additional pressure on the middle infielders, Dick McAuliffe and the new man at shortstop.

"I remember the first play of the first game," Stanley said. "Brock hit me a ground ball, which really took the tension off. I could tell he was choked up a bit at the plate, and he looked like he was trying to hit the ball my way.

"I think that's the biggest mistake they made, because I caught the ball and it took off a lot of the pressure.

"I remember a couple of other plays. Javier hit a ground ball in the hole and I dove and rolled over and lost the ball and he went to second, I got an error on that. I didn't like that. That's the one I remember more than the other one really, the error, given on a diving play. But they had to score it one way or the other."

Twenty years later, Stanley is disputing the scoring decision. "You bet," he said.

✦ ✦ ✦

Whitaker a Tiger of a different stripe

By Joe Falls ✦ *The Detroit News*
ORIGINALLY PRINTED MARCH 5, 1987

S parky Anderson considers him his most talented player. He calls him one of the five best players in baseball. He says he does not see how Charlie Gehringer could have had any more ability than Lou Whitaker, as great as Gehringer was in the old days with the Tigers.

Anderson is as high on Whitaker as any player who has ever played for him.

Yet, he doesn't talk to him, except for an occasional word of encouragement when nobody is looking.

If the manager of the Tigers has to say something to Whitaker, he goes through Coach Dick Tracewski. Anderson believes this is the best way to deal with his second baseman.

"He doesn't like authority — it smothers him," Anderson said Wednesday. "So if I have anything to say to Lou, I tell it to Tracewski. All I ever do is make certain — absolutely certain — that I congratulate him from time to time on how he is playing.

"That, I never miss doing."

It might be in the middle of a game or as they are walking through the tunnel to the field or getting on the team bus after the game, but Anderson will sidle up to Whitaker and say: "You're playing super." They'll talk about family or religion once in a while, but that's the whole relationship between the manager and the second baseman.

It is a distant but not a cool relationship.

Lou Whitaker has been an enigma to the Detroit baseball club for a long time. They see him as a highly-skilled player who has not realized his full potential and may never do so. He can turn out for the first day of spring training and start playing second base like he has never been away. He doesn't need practice.

He looks exactly the same, too. He hasn't aged 30 seconds in 10 years with the Tigers. He is easily the most gifted athlete on the team — a natural when it comes to baseball.

Whitaker says: "I was born to play baseball."

He does not practice as the other players because he doesn't have to.

For one thing, he gets bored. He knows he can do it, so why sweat over it? He can start swinging at curves the first day in camp and slice those liners into left or pull those liners into right. In 1984, he stopped taking batting practice altogether because it became a waste of time and energy. It was coming so easy that batting practice wasn't doing him any good.

The Tigers see this tremendous talent — a player who doesn't have to refine his skills —and they wonder to what extent he could take his game if he fully applied himself. That's their frustration. They see an exceptional player in their midst but one who winds up .281 at the end of the season.

At the same time, they recognize that this man is different than the others. They know he is a man who

✦ ✦ ✦

Lou Whitaker's glovework at second base was golden.

sets his own pace.

Nobody is comfortable talking about it, but this organization has had to make a serious judgment on Lou Whitaker. The Tigers had to decide whether to ask more of him or let him go his way and take what he is able to give. The Tigers chose to let him have free rein.

The other players do not mind it or do not know it. The special treatment is not a problem on this team. Everyone seems to understand Whitaker and his needs. They certainly understand his accomplishments.

The Tigers do not give Whitaker any signs — when to steal, when to hit, when to take. They know it doesn't do much good. He is not interested in such things as signs. He is interested in playing the game his way, and his way is quite often the best way.

He will run when they don't want him to and bunt when they don't want him to bunt. That's frustrating. They always look at the bottom line, and at the bottom line they are satisfied with his numbers.

"He's not a good practicer," Tracewski said. "He has a concentration problem because he is so gifted. He doesn't pay much attention to fundamentals. He doesn't have to. He does them instinctively. He doesn't take batting practice to improve — he takes it just to loosen up. He has such natural ability that he just plays the game as it goes along. He doesn't have to be ready for anything because he can react to everything. He's a reactor.

"It's hard to get to him because he is so quiet and withdrawn. None of us is as close to him as we'd like to be."

Whitaker sat down after Wednesday practice. He was told what others were saying about him — including his rudeness.

"Am I rude?" he said, with a smile. "I guess I am at times. I don't mean to be. I know I can be difficult to get along with. My wife is telling me that all the time. I think maybe I should start changing my ways, I'm certainly old enough to know better. I'll try."

◆ ◆ ◆

Heavily Armed

Dizzy Trout is restrained after almost being beaned by a Boston pitcher.

Jim Bunning   Frank Lary   Dizzy

out   Tommy Bridges   George Mullin

Bunning always ahead of his time

By Joe Falls ✦ *The Detroit News*
ORIGINALLY PRINTED AUGUST 4, 1996

When he is inducted into baseball's Hall of Fame today, Jim Bunning has a point to make. "It's not going to be political, but there are some things I want to say to the game of baseball," Bunning, 64, says. "I want them to know if they don't straighten out their business, the game will cease to exist in the next century."

If baseball is smart, it will pay attention. Jim Bunning has always been ahead of his time. Before most teams began keeping extensive scouting reports on players, Bunning compiled his own book on hitters.

"I had it all in there," Bunning said. "What I did against every batter, what they did against me. Could they hit the slider? Did they like the inside pitch? The big thing I wanted to know is how they reacted with men on base.

"That was the key for me — could they handle the pressure?" Bunning laughed. "Take Willie Mays. He was 100 percent tougher if there was a runner on second base than if he came up with nobody on base. I had to be very careful with him."

Bunning kept track of everything, even the attendance. "You bet," he said. "If we got 5,000 more on the days I pitched, I wanted to know about it."

More important, he wanted his bosses to know about it. He was an agent before there were agents.

"He'd come in with everything, and it was all written down," recalled former Tiger President Jim Campbell, who passed away last year. "I knew how many games he won and lost, and maybe his earned run average. But he could tell me how many runs per

Jim Bunning tossed a no-hitter at Boston in 1958, one of four Tigers to accomplish the feat.

✦ ✦ ✦

Bunning's 224 career victories was good enough to get him into the Hall of Fame in 1996.

each league. When he retired in 1971, he was second to Walter Johnson with 2,885 strikeouts.

He pitched for the Tigers from 1955 through 1963, then went to the National League and pitched six seasons for the Philadelphia Phillies, a year-and-a-half at Pittsburgh and a half-season with the Los Angeles Dodgers.

He went 224-184, and on occasion, could be the most spectacular pitcher in the game. His career earned-run average is 3.27.

Bunning pitched a no-hitter for the Tigers in 1958, getting Ted Williams four times on fly balls in Fenway Park, and then a perfect game for the Phillies against the New York Mets in Shea stadium on Father's Day in 1964.

Bunning went at baseball with everything at his command. He was among the first to show up in the mornings, always the last to leave. He was still running wind sprints when his teammates were teeing it up on the sixth hole.

"Frank Lary had a lot more stuff than I did, and so did Paul Foytack and Billy Hoeft," he said. "I told Foytack that if he applied himself, he could win 20 games every year. But you know Paul. He was a happy go-lucky guy who never got serious. I just wish I had his fastball."

Bunning's sidearm pitches were thrown from the right side with such force that he would fall to the ground with every pitch, landing on his glove. This became his trademark.

Mickey Mantle said Bunning scared him more than any pitcher in the league.

"I was afraid of his stuff — I could never really handle him," Mantle once said.

game our team scored for him — who he beat, when he beat them, the score, the runs, hits and errors.

"When I told him he couldn't have done all those things without the other eight players, he'd laugh and show me more statistics.

"Jim Bunning always got a few more thousand bucks out of me than I wanted to pay him."

Bunning was the first pitcher since Cy Young to win more than 100 games and strike out more than 1,000 in

♦ ♦ ♦

'Yankee Killer' Lary earned the label

By Bill Halls ✦ *The Detroit News*
ORIGINALLY PRINTED AUGUST 5, 1986

"Want to go out and cut some grass?" said the familiar voice over the telephone from Northport, Ala. "Been damn near 95 for two months down here."

There was no mistaking that southern twang. It was Frank Lary, all right. Old Taters. Mule. The Yankee Killer. And, for a while, the best right-handed pitcher in the American League.

"I work some with a county (Tuscaloosa) construction unit," said Lary, who pitched for the Tigers for 10 years (1954-64). "We build roads, cut grass, things like that. My job? I must be a supervisor 'cause I stand in the shade a lot."

Northport is a long outfield throw north of Tuscaloosa, where Lary once pitched for the University of Alabama. He grew up in Northport and came back home after leaving Major League Baseball in the late 1960s. In a 12-year big-league career, Lary won 128 games and lost 116, mostly with average clubs. He had a lifetime earned-run average of 3.49. After leaving the Tigers in 1964, Lary finished his career with the New York Mets, Milwaukee Braves and the Chicago White Sox.

Lary's nicknames all fit him pretty well. Taters was a natural from the time he wrote that word on a railroad dining car menu form (for potatoes) when the Tigers used to travel by train. Mule was the down-home nickname because Lary was strong, which is his middle name. And Yankee Killer doesn't need an explanation.

The New York Yankees, a team that won six pennants between 1955 and 1961, were dog meat when Lary pitched. He was 28-13 lifetime against the Yanks.

"People call me that all the time," said Lary, 56. "'How ya doin,' Yankee Killer?' There's a lot of discussions about baseball down here. Of course, me being a southern boy, I never thought Yankees was too smart. I guess we just outsmarted them."

His throaty laugh was guileless.

"Heck, don't say that. I'll get a bunch of letters. One reason is we played good ball against them. We always made the play at the right time. When one of them got a hit, you don't want to give them the same pitch next time up. When you get on that mound, you want to really concentrate."

Lary remembers a few of those games against the old Yankees of Mickey Mantle, Roger Maris and Bill Skowron.

"I remember hitting a home run off (Tom) Sturdivant and beating them 2-1 once," he said. "Another time, we beat them when I laid down a perfect bunt and Steve Boros scored from third. There were two outs and it was on a two-strike pitch. Old Clete Boyer had backed up at third.

"But the thing I remember most about baseball and Detroit was the fans. They were the best fans I ever played under. Me, being from the South, may have helped. There were a lot of southern people working in those plants up there then. I felt like I was playing at

◆ ◆ ◆

Manager Bucky Harris could always count on Frank Lary to pitch well against the New York Yankees.

home with the Tigers. I really enjoyed the fans."

Lary twice won 20 games for the Tigers. He was 21-13 in 1956 and he was 23-9 in 1961. After that, Lary got a sore arm, whether pitching when it was too cold, or pitching with a leg injury. At any rate, he won only six more games for the Tigers, was traded to the New York Mets in 1964 and was finished by 1965.

"Chuck Dressen and I didn't get along," said Lary. "Nobody can pitch if they're out of the regular rotation."

After retiring while with the White Sox, Lary took a job as minor-league pitching coach with the Mets.

"I had Tom Seaver, Tug McGraw, Nolan Ryan and Jerry Koosman," said Lary. "Just a few rinky dinks." More laughter.

"I don't feel like the boys have got their minds really on the game nowadays. We played for the fun of it. Nolan Ryan makes as much in one ballgame as I made in one season. I guess my top salary was $40,000 back in '61 when I won 23 games."

After coaching a couple of years in the minors, Lary quit baseball for good and went back to Northport. He ran an ice cream business for awhile and later was elected, as a Democrat, to a term on the Tuscaloosa County Board of Revenue.

❖ ❖ ❖

Trout won the hearts of Tigers, fans

By **Jerry Green** ◆ *The Detroit News*
ORIGINALLY PRINTED FEBRUARY 29, 1972

There was a different breed of rookie showing up in the spring training camps of Florida 35 years ago. In that era, the rookies didn't bring much sophistication with them. Certainly, they had no moneybags, like the rookies of today. They rode into town in jalopies, if they owned an automobile at all.

Lots of them were homespun, milk-fed farmboys who had served their lengthy apprenticeships in places such as Beaumont or Rocky Mount or Indianapolis. Many of them had quaint names: Rabbit, Gabby or Diz.

It was 35 years ago just this week that a strapping rookie reported to the Detroit Tigers' spring camp in Lakeland.

"I'm Paul Howard Trout, of Terre Haute, Ind." announced the 21-year-old, right-handed pitcher to the club manager, Mickey Cochrane.

"Paul H. Trout, but they call me Diz," said the talkative rookie to a bellboy in the New Florida Hotel. "It ain't because I've got as much stuff as Diz Dean but they call me Diz because I talk as much as Diz Dean. Anyway, everybody says I do. So you can call me Diz." Dizzy Trout, up from Indianapolis, didn't stick with the Tigers that first year, 1937. But later Trout was to pitch in two World Series and in tandem with Hal Newhouser to supply some of the finest excitement in the baseball history of Detroit.

Trout won 170 games and lost 61 in a big league career that extended from 1939 through 1952. He spent all but part of his final season with Detroit — and he was a legendary figure.

In 1944 the Tigers lost the pennant on the final day. But Newhouser won 29 games and Trout 27.

"He was an extremely marvelous man," said Newhouser.

"He had a heart as big as an elephant. He shared everything with everybody.

"We shared a record that won't be broken in a long time," continued Newhouser. "Diz won 27 games in 1944 and I won 29. Between us we broke the Dean Brothers' record (Dizzy and Paul's 49 aggregate in 1934). We were in 96 games of the 154 that year.

"Diz would pitch one day and I'd pitch the next and then we'd hope it would rain."

In 1944, Trout lost the final game of the season to Washington and the Tigers lost the pennant by a game to the St. Louis Browns.

"If we'd had nine pitchers like him, we'd never have lost," said Newhouser.

"One of the biggest thrills was winning in the World Series in 1945. I won the seventh game against the Cubs. But if he didn't win the sixth, we'd lost the World Series right then. He won the most important game of the Series."

Trout was a humorous and sometimes profane after-dinner speaker. He also had a belligerent temper

Trout, second from left, has a few fish stories for his teammates in 1952. From left, Frank House, Trout, Ted Lyons, Rick Ferrell, Johnny Groth and Ted Gray.

and had occasional spats with fans and teammates. One memorable picture of Trout shows him grabbing a box seat heckler by the shirt. Trout engaged in occasional battles, once with his manager, Del Baker, once with Hank Greenberg, and once even with Newhouser in the Tigers' dugout.

Diz and his wife, Pearl, had 10 children. He spent most of his adult life as a resident of Detroit, and for a while after he retired as a player he helped broadcast Tiger games with Van Patrick.

At his death, Trout was a member of the Chicago White Sox organization. He joined them in 1959 as a pitching instructor. Later he became a member of their public relations corps, traveling about and speaking at banquets.

Occasionally he tried to enter politics, but never quite made it. Once he was defeated in an election to become sheriff of Wayne County.

But he was a winner more often than not as a pitcher. With 170 victories in his career, he won five more games than Sandy Koufax and 20 more that Dizzy Dean.

◆ ◆ ◆

Bridges made his mark in 16 seasons

The Detroit News staff
Originally printed April 6, 1976

They called him "Little T from Tennessee." That was Tommy Bridges, who spent his entire 16-year major-league career in a Tiger uniform. When he departed in 1946 at age 39 he had a 194-138 won-lost record.

Sixty-six of those victories came in 1934-36, at the height of his career. He led the American League twice in strikeouts, posted a 4-1 World Series record and was the winning pitcher in the 1939 All-Star game.

The tiny Tennesseean was to say later he wished he could have won 195 games. He could have added his World Series and All-Star decisions for an even 200.

Although never weighing more than 160 pounds in his playing day, Bridges came to the Tigers in 1930 after setting a strikeout record in the minors with a strike-out record in the minors with a blazing fastball and curve some shouldn't believe.

"Have you ever watched a ball roll across the table, then fall to the floor?," one player asked. "If so, you've seen Bridges' curve."

Bridges averaged 100 strikeouts a season for Detroit. One year he struck out 175.

The whiff he wanted, but didn't get, was Dave Harris in a 1932 game against the Washington Senators.

With two out in the ninth and the Detroiters leading 13-0, pinch hitter Harris slapped a fastball to left field for a single — the game's first and only hit off Bridges. It ruined a perfect game.

"Little T" didn't regret not throwing his trusty curve. He was, he said following his game plan of setting up the batter with a fastball, then coming in with the hook.

They wanted Bridges to be a doctor. His father is a doctor and his grandfather was one. He started studying medicine and quit. He studied literature and became a baseball player. He mixed curves, fastballs and the classics.

"I have been throwing baseballs every since I can remember, ever since I could walk," he said. "I love to throw. Baseball has been good to me. It has given me many advantages and many opportunities that would never have come my way had I studied medicine and become a doctor, or studied law and become a lawyer, or gone into business."

At season's end, Bridges always returned to Gordonville, Tenn. — population 400 — where his father still practiced medicine.

He always liked the place.

"When I arrive home in October, the hunting season is about to start and each fall I go hunting with the same group of men. We've been doing it for years and I like it because we just hunt and none of them ever mention baseball. I guess they've never seen a ball game."

Bridges had many great moments in a Tigers uniform, but his best was his first.

"The biggest thrill that I ever had in baseball happened on the day that I pitched for Detroit for the first time. It was in New York and I was sent in as a relief pitcher. As I walked to the box the catcher came down

Tommy Bridges Day on September 7, 1941.

to me and said, 'Now, when Ruth and Gehrig come to bat, just remember that they're nothing but two more ballplayers and just pitch to them.' I said, 'all right,' but when I looked up, who was strolling to the plate but Ruth and he looked like two parts of the Himalayan Mountain range to me. I have never seen anything bigger or more ponderous and massive looking moving toward home plate.

"I bore down on Ruth and he hit a fast grounder to Gehringer and was thrown out. But that wasn't the end for me. Gehrig was coming up and here was an

even bigger menace than Ruth because Gehrig was in a great batting streak at the time. Well, I struck out Gehrig and when I saw him swing for the third time and miss I had a thrill that nothing since has equaled. My blood tingled for 10 minutes afterward, and as long as I live I'll never forget that moment."

In 1947, Bridges, who was inducted into the Michigan Hall of Fame in 1963, finally pitched that no-hitter — for Portland in the Pacific Coast League. He was 40, and was to go on pitching in the minors until the age of 43.

✦ ✦ ✦

Mullin was a brainiac on the mound

By H.G. Salsinger ✦ *The Detroit News*
Originally printed January 10, 1944

T here will be no niche in baseball's hall of fame at Cooperstown, N. Y., for the late George Mullin, and his name will not be included in the all-time list of great pitchers. But in the light of present-day pitching, Mullin's work over a five-year span was extraordinary.

From 1905 until 1909 he averaged better than 21 victories a season. He compiled a 108-78 record, good for a .527 winning percentage.

In three of those years he won more than 20 games, while only three pitchers won 20 or more. Few pitchers in the last two decades have matched Mullin's 1909 record of 29-8.

Mullin had an excellent fast ball and a good curve but most of his success was due to smartness rather than stuff. He had a great many tricks, some of which not only drove opposing batters to distraction, but annoyed the home folks as well.

Mullin and Eddie Plank used the same tactics to make the batter over-anxious. George would paw around the pitcher's box whenever a dangerous batter stood at the plate. He would loosen his belt or tighten it. He would remove his cap and find some imaginary thing wrong, something that he would have to fix immediately.

He would tie his shoe laces, or even take off a shoe. He would reshape his glove and remove imaginary dirt.

While this was going on the crowd became impatient, and some of the ill-bred among the customers would begin shouting vulgar comments and advice. George has what the profession calls "rabbit ears,"

meaning that he was sensitive to nay criticisms from the stands. Secretly, he undoubtedly welcomed them for it aided his act. It gave him an opportunity to engage in repartee with the customers.

He would tell them what he thought of them, and they would tell him what they thought of him, and so it went back and forth while the batter got more and more nervous and anxious.

That was the purpose of the whole performance. When the batter became so enraged and disgusted that he would swing at anything, Mullin threw him a bad ball. He solved many situations in that way. So did Plank.

They were never any more popular with the customers than with opposing players, but this didn't bother them as long as they achieved their purpose, which was getting rid of the batters.

Mullin and his battery-mate, Charlie Schmidt, once saved a game with a wild pitch, as odd an example of pitching strategy as you are likely to meet in any age of baseball.

Detroit was playing New York and it was a tight ball game. Jack Chesbro was pitching for the Highlanders (as the New York team was known at the time) and Mullin for Detroit.

They were playing at the old American League park

✦ ✦ ✦

George Mullin started and won both ends of a doubleheader in 1906.

in New York and going into the last half of the ninth, Detroit was leading 1-0. An error put the first New York batter on base, a sacrifice sent him to second, and an infield out got him to third. New York's best hitter was up.

Schmidt called for time and walked out to the pitcher's box. He told Mullin:

"Here's what you do: Fire that ball as hard as you can over my head. Then you run to the plate. This guy on third will try to score. I'll retrieve the ball and throw to you and you tag him when he comes sliding in."

Mullin thought over the suggestion for a moment.

"I think you're crazy, but I'm willing to gamble, and if you don't make the play I'll bust that thick skull of yours with a bat."

Mullin threw the next pitch over Schmidt's head. As Schmidt turned to pursue the ball the runner broke from third and Mullin ran to the plate. The ball hit the stands and, luckily, shot back on a straight line to Schmidt, who had not considered the possibility of a bounce in any direction but the right one. Schmidt grabbed the ball, tossed it to Mullin, and Mullin tagged the runner five feet from the plate ending the game.

"That's was a smart idea of mine wasn't it?" said Schmidt to Mullin as they walked off the field.

"It's so smart that we'll never try it again," Mullin told him, and they never did.

◆ ◆ ◆

Sparky Anderson tips his hat to the Baltimore crowd before his final game in 1995.

Acknowledgements

Our vivid recollections of the players and field generals who have worn the "old English D" have been captured through the years in stories and photographs in the *Detroit News*, many of them reproduced in this book. The fine works of the writers and photographers have made baseball an enjoyable experience that Detroiters have shared through the years.

The writers contributing to this book include Jerry Green, Joe Falls, George Cantor, Lynn Henning, Tom Gage, H.G. Salsinger, Doc Greene, Mike O'Hara, Bill Brennan, Larry Middlemas, Bob Wojnowski, Sam Green, Angelique S. Chengelis and Watson Spoelstra.

The photographers, whose images bring these pages to life, include William Kuenzel, Monroe D. Stroecker, Milton Brooks, William Seiter, Rolland Ransom, Don Walker, James Kilpatrick, Peter A. MacGregor, Edwin C. Lombardo, Drayton Holcomb, Duane Belanger, William T. Anderson, Robert Coon, Michael S. Green, Kirthmon Dozier, David C. Coates, Alan Lessig, Dale G. Young, Steve Haines and Charles V. Tines.

◆ ◆ ◆